SURVIVING THE CLAWS OF THE TIGER

FOXTROT'S FIGHT FOR SURVIVAL IN OPERATION UNION II
JUNE 2, 1967 - VIETNAM

John Gobrecht
Foxtrot 2/5 2nd Platoon

Foreword by
Colonel Benedict Laurence
U.S. Army Retired

Copyright © 2013 John William Gobrecht

All rights reserved. No part of this book may be reproduced without written permission of the author or the publisher except; with proper credit, brief quotations may be used within the scope of current Copyright Law.

Cover Design by John W. Gobrecht
Book Design and layout by Sally Gobrecht

Front Cover images:
Vietnam Campaign Ribbon, Vietnam Service Ribbon, Presidential Unit Citation Ribbon, Purple Heart Medal with Gold Star and Dog Tags.

ISBN-13: 978-1492104056

Dedication

Dedicated to the Corpsmen and Marines of Union II who gave the ultimate, life itself.

Soldier

I was that which others did not want to be.

I went where others feared to go, and did what others failed to do.

I asked nothing from those who gave nothing, and reluctantly accepted the thought of eternal loneliness ... should I fail.

I have seen the face of terror; felt the stinging cold of fear; and enjoyed the sweet taste of a moment's love.

I have cried, pained and hoped ...but most of all, I have lived times others would say were best forgotten.

At least someday I will be able to say that I was proud of what I was ... a soldier.

By George L. Skypeck

With permission of George L. Skypeck, Reg. TM, Copyright All Rights Reserved

Acknowledgments

My sincere thanks to family and friends who encouraged me to put into print the experience the marines of Union II endured in June of 1967.

I would like to thank individually the people who aided me in the long and tedious process of publishing this document listed in alphabetical order are: Todd Bollinger, John Coulson, Frankie Gobrecht, Sally Gobrecht, Terry Gobrecht, Ali Gruver, Pennie Gruver, Benedict (Ben) Laurence (Colonel, U.S. Army Retired), Christa Laurence, John Markle, Penny Miller, Demi Stevens, along with the *Year of the Book*, Paul Smith Library of Southern York County and Joyce Wentz.

Three marines I would also like to recognize are: Louis Rick Barnes, David Brown (Lieutenant Colonel, Retired), and the late Perry Jerry Jones for the added information missing in my files.

Three people needing further recognition are Sally Gobrecht, Ben Laurence and Demi Stevens.

Sally donated innumerable hours formatting and editing my writings into book form and prepared it for the final step before publishing. Without her expertise, my document would have gone nowhere.

Ben, a long time friend who had worked for USA Today Newspaper for many years and is also a retired Colonel of the United States Army, volunteered to write the foreword for my book. It was greatly appreciated.

Demi went the extra yard to teach and answer any questions I asked of her. She did this with patience and professionalism. I cannot thank her enough.

I would also like to give thanks for the privilege and opportunity to fight alongside the men of Fox Company, 2nd Battalion, 5th Marine Regiment of the 1st Marine Division. Their courage and sacrifice is what motivated me to write this book.

Lastly, I want to praise the United States Marine Corps for the excellent training before and during my tour in Vietnam. They taught me to think things through and stay calm, even during life and death situations and concentrate on survival.

The esprit de corps kicks in during critical situations. We either fight to live or fight and die. Surrender is never an option. Thanks to the Corps.

I learned that even though Marines die, their regiment remains immortal.

SEMPER FIDELIS

Contents

Foreword	i
Introduction	1
Destined for Vietnam	5
The Que Son Basin's Value to the Enemy	7
Known Operations in the Que Son Valley	11
Units of Union II	14
Prelude to Battle: Operation Union Kicks Off	19
May 1 - The Bloodbath Begins	21
Operation Union II: Unit Coordination	25
May 26 - Meeting the Enemy Head-on	27
May 30 - Fox Company Mobilizes	29
May 31 - Snipers are Neutralized	31
June 1 - The Calm before the Storm	33
June 2 - Fox Company steps into Hell	35
June 2 - The Annihilation of 2nd Platoon	43
June 2 - Surviving the Counter Attack	47
June 2 - Night Escape	55
June 3 - The Ups and Downs of Rescue	59
Area Marine is Wounded Second Time	65
June 3 - Hospital Recovery	67
Casualties of Operation Union II	75
Citations	81
Medal of Honor Recipients	85
Fallen Soldier Table	93
Letters	95
Bibliography	101

Glossary of Terms and Abbreviations 105
Notes 111
U. S. Marine Corps Chain of Command 113
Index 115

Maps

Ho Chi Minh Trail Network
I Corps - The Northern Province 3
Major MAF Operations.. 8
Operation Union II Nui Loc Son Basin
    Action of 30 May - 2 June 32
Union II 1200 Hours 36
Rice Paddy Assault 37
Counter Attack..50

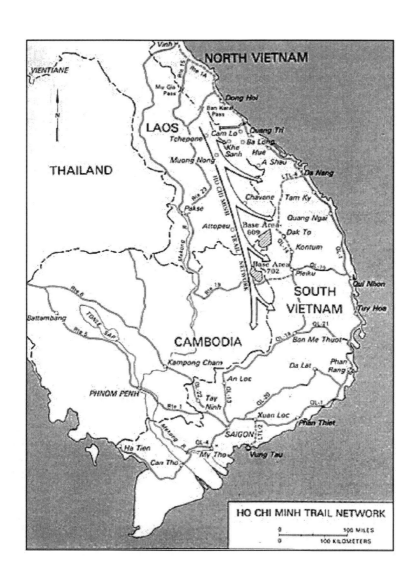

Foreword

Make no mistake about what you are about to read. This content is the author's personal account of what happened to him and his team during one of the bloodiest single-day battles of the Vietnam War. It took place at the Battle of the Que Son Valley during Operation Union II in the summer of 1967.

What happened in the blink of an eye has affected the author's life every hour of every day since then. His enduring effort to save himself and others from the enemy all around him that day has constantly raised the question: "Why am I still here today?"

The author has spent enumerable hours since that tragic battle trying to understand and to explain what happened.

John Gobrecht, the author, has made it clear to me that his writing should not be perceived in any way as him focusing on himself. Rather, he is telling his story so the reader can be better informed of what John and his comrades had to endure, while fighting in Vietnam — it is their story as seen through John.

I did ask John's permission to provide a very short perspective as I remember him during those years before he was a soldier.

I knew him best as Johnny, the kid. His parents and my parents were best friends. Since Johnny was a few years younger than me, we initially crossed paths during family gatherings. Each of us was the oldest son of the family, but my siblings included two younger brothers while Johnny's siblings included four brothers and four sisters. This was an unusually large family, even during the period of the 50's and the 60's. This large family was really unique in the way all of the family members worked together in absolute harmony. I was always amazed watching each of them pulling together to accomplish whatever was required for the good of the family. They were all genuine in their effort to support their parents and their siblings. Each person determined the family's needs and then took pride in their accomplishments. There wasn't conflict, but helpful cooperation. The Gobrecht family was impressive and respected in their community.

Johnny and I were both football players in high school. Since he was a few years younger, he had the daily opportunity to go up against the older and the bigger players. Bigger for sure — because at that time in his life Johnny was small. In appearance, you would immediately say to yourself that he should not be out there playing against those relative giants. It was nothing to Johnny. He earned the respect of all the players very quickly. He would tackle any task and any player, always. He played much bigger than his physical size and he played well. He never backed down, always courageous.

In my opinion, these are just two examples of many experiences from his youth that prepared him to succeed in Vietnam. His personal inner strength, his "can do" attitude, and his compassion for others have always been evident in Johnny. I believe that's why he is still here today.

Benedict E Laurence

Col Retired U.S. Army

Introduction

The Vietnam War was a fact of life for many people during the turbulent 60's and early 70's. The war was frowned upon by the peace lovers and backed solidly by the people whose business ventures were making them rich. Many of us young soldiers sent to fight the war were caught in the middle of this political tug of war. TV portrayed us as killers and druggies, exhilarating in the destruction of this ancient, beautiful land.

The fighting wasn't exhilarating, but exhausting and deadly. It wasn't only deadly physically, but also emotionally; creating a void within your person that eventually blocks out all sense of caring and compassion. We did as we were told, and we did it well, with only minor complaining. We were always too tired, but managed to go into battle with confidence that we were doing the right thing.

One battle in particular needs telling; the battle for the Que Son Basin, Operation Union II. It was a time in the Vietnam War when the Viet Cong political structure was beginning to wane and the political arm of Ho Chi Minh (then current leader of North Vietnam) was stretching all the way south to the Delta country of South Vietnam. The large number of North Vietnamese troops moving south in 1967 was proof enough that something big was in the offing. That big event would occur in 1968 and be known as the "Tet Offensive".

Due to these large North Vietnamese enemy troop movements into the south, major tactical operations were set in motion by the U.S. and South Vietnamese military in an effort to disrupt the enemy's plans. One of these tactical operations was named Operation Union II which was launched May 26, 1967.

The unit (Fox 2/5) to which I was assigned at that time was directly involved in this operation. Ultimately, it was my unit of Fox 2/5's 2nd Platoon that was hardest hit during this operation. In fact, at the end of the battle, my assigned company suffered eighty-six casualties. It proved to be the heaviest fighting for my assigned Regiment (the 5th Marines) since their arrival in Vietnam in April, 1966. In the end, the Que Son Basin in 1967 proved to be the bloodiest battle site during the entire war in Vietnam.

These battles were so bloody that they were referred to over thirty years later by former U.S. Marine Otto J. Lehrack (from page 1 of his book, "Road of 10,000 Pains"). In 1999, while he was touring embattled Vietnam, he and other U.S. Marines accompanied by North Vietnamese Army and Viet Cong veterans — during dinner one Viet Cong veteran calmly declared, "Oh yes, in the Que Son Valley in 1967, we killed more Americans than at any time or place during the war". Operation Union II was one such battle. I feel compelled to tell you about it from my own personal perspective.

I have tried to focus only on those events affecting my company's personnel. I have tried to put together all the information I could gather up to this time, knowing full well there is still more to be uncovered. I always felt it a privilege to have been part of such a close knit group of men. Through my writing, I hope to shed some light on the hardships that we experienced as a military unit during those days of May and June, 1967.

I decided on the title for this book from the strategy prophesied by the great, but brutal General Giap, referred to as, "The Tiger". He commanded the communist troops of North and South Vietnam. *His philosophy was to "grab the enemy by the belt", so close as to make artillery and air power ineffactual. You use the stealth of the tiger to move in close and then charge to kill your prey. They did it well, especially in Operation Union II.

*Currey, 257

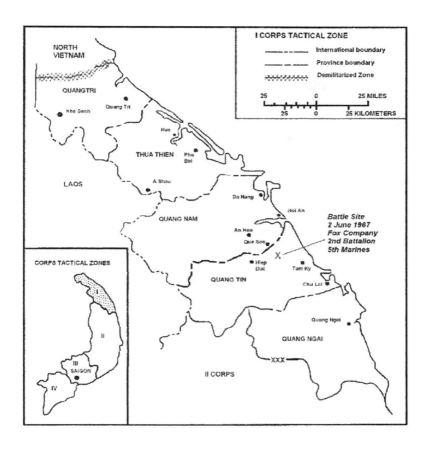

Destined for Vietnam

Upon graduation from South Western High School in Hanover, Pennsylvania in May of 1964, I found myself ready for my next step in life - college. I was in my third semester when I decided to leave school and on February 17, 1966, enlisted in the Marine Corps. It seems so ironic that in January 1966 I was a college student, and by July of that same year I was a machine gunner, fighting in the Vietnam War at the age of nineteen. The Vietnam War had been escalating dramatically since 1965, and within six months of my enlistment I found myself on an aircraft bound for Da Nang, Vietnam by way of Japan and Okinawa.

On July 27, 1966 I began my combat tour in the People's Republic of Vietnam, after my International flight landed at 1430 hours at the massive airbase in Da Nang.

I spent my first night in Vietnam manning a perimeter bunker at the Da Nang airstrip. The next morning I boarded a CH-34 Marine helicopter which took me twenty-five miles southwest of the airbase to the area of An Hoa. This is where my assigned unit was located. I was to be a machine gunner for 2nd Platoon, India Company. We were part of the 3rd Battalion, Ninth Marine Regiment (3/9) of the 3rd Marine Division.

Our Tactical Area of Responsibility (TAOR) included the An Hoa Basin, the Arizona Valley (Indian Country), Son Thu Bon Valley, Song Vu Gia Valley, Antenna Valley, Cu Ban Area, My Loc 2 and Phu Lac 6 outposts, Liberty Bridge and adjacent areas of Hill 55.

Our encounters were mostly with units of the Viet Cong (VC), sometimes led by smaller units of North Vietnamese Army Regulars

(NVA). The area contained hundreds, if not thousands, of booby-traps, miles of tunnel systems and many snipers.

In December 1966, my assigned unit, 3/9, moved to the northern I Corp area. However, I did not personally move with them. Instead I was reassigned to the unit that replaced 3/9. It was the 2nd Battalion, 5th Marine Regiment (2/5) of the 1st Marine Division. I was now a member of 2nd Platoon, Fox Company, because they had a serious shortage of machine gunners. I remained assigned to 2/5 for the remainder of my days in Vietnam.

This was my destiny — to remain in the An Hoa area to be directly involved in one of the deadliest American battles of the war, Operation Union II — The Battle for the Que Son Basin.

The Que Son Basin's Value to the Enemy

Strategic Value:

South Vietnam is divided into four distinct areas or corps. Northern area is I Corps, which borders North Vietnam to the north, the country of Laos to the west and through the Province of Quang Ngai to the south. Southwest of Da Nang is the area known as the Que Son Basin.

Control of this densely populated Que Son Basin area was essential to the Communists, not only for the food supplies and rest areas, but also for the striking capabilities of the NVA 2nd Division against such targets as Da Nang to the northeast, An Hoa's industrial complex to the north, Tam Ky to the east and Chu Lai to the south.

Before the arrival of the U.S. Marines, the only resistance to the NVA's 2nd Division was the Army of the Republic of Vietnam's (ARVN) outpost at Nui Loc Son. When U.S. Army forces arrived within this southern I Corps area it released U.S. Marine units to become engaged in major large scale operations and to reinforce the ARVN compound.

Certain intelligence reports confirmed that the NVA 2nd Division located in the Basin was also being supplied with fresh troops and supplies from North Vietnam via the Ho Chi Minh Trail. Other intelligence established that the North Vietnamese considered control of the Que Son Basin critical at "whatever costs".

A high ranking Communist officer, Colonel Haynh Cu, who surrendered to III Marine Amphibious Force (III MAF) in early March 1967, stated that the Que Son Basin would be a major objective for the

NVA. Their campaign was scheduled to begin during the month of April. (Refer to pg. 1 1 1 Notes for more info.)

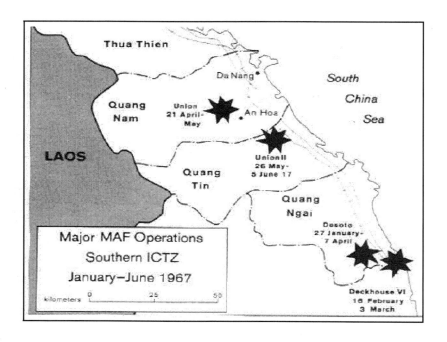

Geographic Value:

"Que Son/Que Son Basin is basically one and the same as Nui Loc Son/Nui Loc Son Basin. This entire area is known as the Hiep Duc – Que Son – Thang Binh Corridor", an agriculturally rich piece of geography. This area was strategically important for various reasons, some being that: it contained a large population, it was a large rice producing area and it was a major source of salt.*

The Basin extends for about forty kilometers from Route 1 all the way to Hiep Duc. It is bordered by mountains on the north, south, and west. The Ly Ly River and Routes 534 and 535 each run through the center of the area. This corridor, lying on the border of Quang Nam and Quang Tin Provinces is situated some twenty-five kilometers northwest of Tam Ky.

*Salt had traditionally been a medium of barter and a taxable commodity in Vietnam. Moreover, the hot climate, of Vietnam makes its use a dietary necessity.

Some 60, 000 Vietnamese reside in this basin and had been under control of the Communists for some twenty-five years, making this a very volatile area for invading U.S. forces.

Friendly Allied Strategy:

U.S. and ARVN forces planned to disrupt and take control of the Que Son Basin because U.S. intelligence reports confirmed the importance of this area to the enemy. So, in 1967, major operations in the Que Son Basin began with Operation Union which took place in April and early May of that year.

Operation Union exacted a large toll on the 2nd NVA Division, but not nearly enough for them to abandon their objective to control the Que Son Basin. Frequent skirmishes soon after Operation Union, substantiated reports that the 3rd and 21st NVA regiments were again moving back into the basin. These enemy units were thought to have moved into this area from Northern II Corps.

The success of Union resulted in the planning of a follow-up operation in the Que Son Basin shortly thereafter. This follow-up operation was code name Union II, and is where I will experience the hell of combat.

Known Operations In The Que Son Basin

Operation Harvest Moon: December 8-20, 1965

A search and destroy operation involving units from the 7th, 3rd, 9th and 4th Marine Regiments. Also accompanying the Marines were several South Vietnam ARVN and Ranger Battalions. The main purpose was to make contact with three battalions of Viet Cong causing havoc in the area of the Que Son Valley. Large amounts of weapons and supplies were captured, while 407 of the enemy were killed and thirty-three captured. Friendly forces also paid a price, losing forty-five Marines killed and 218 wounded. South Vietnamese losses were ninety killed, ninety-one missing and 141 wounded. Valuable lessons on air-ground coordination would be augmented in future operations. It also proved that American fighting men could stand toe to toe with the enemy during the muddy and rainy monsoon season.

Operation Double Eagle II: February 19-March 1, 1966

A search and destroy operation executed by units of the 7th, 9th and 1st Marine Regiments. No large enemy units were encountered, but twenty-eight tons of rice, 500 pounds of sweet potatoes, fifty-three weapons and 450 rounds of ammunition were captured or destroyed. Enemy dead were 125 with fifteen more captured, while Marines suffered six killed and another 136 wounded. The operation was considered a failure.

Operation Kansas: June 16-23, 1966

The offensive was basically a 1st Force Reconnaissance with assistance from Echo Company of the 2nd Battalion, 5th Marine Regiment in support of a B-52 Arc Light Strike in a known area used by the 2nd NVA Division in the Que Son Valley. Following the B-52 strikes there were eighty-five enemy dead, forty elephants, and ten water buffalo littering the area. Marines suffered nine dead and twenty wounded. Because of the constant reconnaissance artillery fire, it prevented enemy troops from massing into large units.

Operation Colorado: August 6-15, 1966

A search and destroy mission requiring the 1st Battalion, 5th Marine Regiment to sweep areas north and west of Tam Ky to route any hidden Viet Cong (VC) in the vicinity. A North Vietnamese Command Post was destroyed. Thirty of the enemy were killed and thirty-five wounded; seven Marines were killed and another twenty-seven wounded.

Operation Union: April 21 to May 16, 1967

A search and destroy operation in the Que Son Valley, carried out by the 1st and 5th Marine Regiments. The object of the operation was the 2nd Division of the Peoples Army of Vietnam (PAVN) or North Vietnamese Army (NVA). Marine units suffered 100 killed, two missing and 473 wounded, while the enemy suffered 865 killed of which 486 were of the NVA 2nd Division. The operation fractured the enemy forces, but left them still viable as a fighting force.

Operation Union II: May 26-June 5, 1967

A search and destroy operation in the Que Son Valley, carried out by the 5th Marine Regiment against the 2nd North Vietnamese Army (NVA) Division. The U.S. forces reported the NVA lost 594 killed and twenty-three captured, while U.S. casualties were 110 killed and 241 wounded. Enemy forces were so decimated that they would not be a factor in the area for months to come, until reinforcements arrived via the Ho Chi Minh Trail from North Vietnam.

Operation Cochise: August 11-28, 1967

A 1st Marine Division Task Force X-ray search and destroy operation enlisting units from the 5th and 11th Marine Regiments in the area of Quang Nam and Quang Tin Provinces. The offensive's main objective was to make contact with the 2nd North Vietnamese Army Division (NVA) and destroy its suspected logistical base somewhere in the area. Enemy casualties were 156 killed with thirteen more captured. Marines suffered ten killed and ninety-three wounded. Even though the 2nd NVA Division would temporarily abandon the area, they wouldn't be gone for long.

Operation Swift: September 4-15, 1967

A military operation involving the 1st Marine Division, whose main purpose was the rescue of two Marine companies which had previously been ambushed by the North Vietnamese Army. The ensuing offensive killed 127 Marines and an estimated 600 North Vietnamese. Despite their withdrawal after having suffered much higher losses, the NVA had accomplished their objective of intercepting an American offensive operation and inflicting many casualties. The NVA had a strategic victory, while the U.S. forces won a tactical victory.

Operation Wheeler/Wallowa: Sept. 11 – Nov. 11, 1967

A search and destroy and security operation by the Army's 1st Brigade and 2nd Squadron, 11th Armored Calvary Regiment, 23rd Infantry Division and 3rd Battalion, 1st Calvary in Quang Nam and Quang Tin Provinces. In all the consolidation of Operations Wheeler and Wallowa netted 3,188 of the enemy killed, eighty-seven captured, plus 743 weapons seized. U.S. Army losses were 258 killed and another 1,190 wounded.

Units of Union II

Allies

ARVN Forces I Corps – Lieutenant General Hoang Xuam Lam
    (ARVN – Army of the Republic of Vietnam)
    2nd ARVN Division
        6th ARVN Regiment
        1st ARVN Ranger Group

U.S. MARINES

III MAF – Lieutenant General Louis W. Walt
    (III Marine Amphibious Force)
    3rd Marine Division – Major General Bruno A. Hochmath
    1st MAW – Major General Louis B. Robertshaw
        (Marine Aircraft Wing)
    1st Force Reconnaissance Company – Captain Albert K. Dixon II
        Sting Ray Patrol – Team Classmate
    1st Marine Division – Major Donn J. Robertson
        5th Marine Regiment – Colonel Houghton
            1st Battalion (maneuver groups for III MAF)
            1st Battalion – Colonel Hilgartner
                ALPHA Company
                DELTA Company
                HEADQUARTERS – Captain James Graham
            2nd Battalion (assigned to 1st Battalion)
                FOX Company – Captain James Graham (assigned)
                    1st Platoon – 2nd Lieutenant Charles Joseph Schultz
                    2nd Platoon – 2nd Lieutenant Straughan D. Kelsey, Jr.
                    3rd Platoon – 1st Lieutenant James B. Scuras
            3rd Battalion (maneuver groups for III MAF)
            3rd Battalion – Lieutenant Colonel Esslinger
                    Lieutenant Colonel Webster (later)
                INDIA Company
                LIMA Company
                MIKE Company
    1st Division Reserves – Lieutenant Colonel Jackson
        5th Marine Regiment
            2nd Battalion
                ECHO Company

7th Marine Regiment
   1st Battalion
      DELTA Company
   2nd Battalion
      ECHO Company
   (reserves eventually assigned and activated

Enemy Units

NVA – General Vo Nguyen Giap
   (North Vietnamese Army)
     2nd NVA Division – Major General Hoang Thoa
        3rd NVA Regiment
        21st NVA Regiment
        31st NVA Regiment
        3rd Viet Cong Regiment
        1st Viet Cong Regiment
        (arrives August 9, 1967)

Propaganda Leaflets Distributed by the VC

+ WELCOME TO GENUINE AMERICANS WHO, FOR THE SAKE OF DEMOCRACY AND FREEDOM IDEALS, OPPOSE THE U S GOVERNMENT'S DIRTY WAR IN SOUTH VIETNAM.

+ STOP TERRORIST RAIDS, MASSACRE, PLUNDER, HOUSE BURNING, WOMEN RAPING.

Your people are praying to Christ for your safety as you often do for the happiness of your family not to be shattered by this unjust war.

But Johnson keeps sending more and more troops to South Vietnam and is stepping up his criminal war of aggression and the death toll of U.S. troops is rising s eadly here.

American servicemen

Don't fire at and spray suffocating gas into our people's air and cannon shelters.

Don't destroy crop, kill domestic animals and plunder our people's property.

Repression, terrorism, massacre, house burning, women raping... are not the democratic American's ideals.

Stop spraying noxious chemicals in South Vietnam.

Stop the war of aggression in South Vietnam ! bloods of American and Vietnamese Youths have been shed too much !

Peace in South Vietnam and repatriation of all U.S. troops !

THE SOUTH VIETNAM NATIONAL FRONT
FOR LIBERATION

U.S. OFFICERS AND MEN !

In former times, your ancestors heroically opposed British impe - rialism to realize independence, freedom to the Americans. That was a just war, approved by the American people and suppoted by the world's people.

To - day, you come to South Vietnam to carry out Johnson - Mac Namara's war of aggression, countering the Vietnamese people's dispirations for independence and freedom. This is an injust war, in contrast with the freedom - and - justice - loving traditions of the American people, in contrast with the progressive spirit of mankind in the warld.

It's the reason why all American people and the peace - loving people the world over ceaselessly protested against and condemned this derty war.

- STOP TERRORIST RAIDS, MASSACRE, PLUNDER, HOUSE-BURNING AND WOMEN-RAPING!
- REPATRIATION OF ALL U.S. TROOPS!
- PEACE FOR VIETNAM!

Prelude to Battle: Operation Union Kicks Off

The Que Son Basin first became an important issue, while I was recuperating from a bullet wound aboard the hospital ship, *Sanctuary*. We had been enroute to the Philippines when we were notified to return to the Vietnam coast line, between Da Nang and Chu Lai near the coastal city of Tam Ky. Operation Union was in progress and heavy casualties were expected. Union II would be next.

Author on a machine gun bunker, fourteen miles west of An Hoa at Nong Son (coal mine) overlooking Antenna Valley, a major infiltration route for the North Vietnamese Army.

May 1 - The Bloodbath Begins

While on the hospital ship, we received word that the large Marine operation, code name Union, was in progress and we would be receiving a large number of casualties.

It was evening when we began receiving the Ch-46-A helicopters known as Sea Knights, mede-vacing in the wounded. Due to severe battle damage, one of these large choppers was having trouble remaining airborne. She was coming in too low to make the bow and ditched approximately fifty meters from the ship. The Sea Knight remained afloat for only a very short time before sinking and taking with her most of the occupants. The pilot helped in rescuing a few of the wounded, but he too was eventually lost.

I remember how relieved I was for not being a participant in Union.

About ten days prior to the start of Union II, I left the hospital ship and returned to the battalion area of An Hoa. We remained in the area performing the normal tasks of patrolling, sweeping, ambushing and even the lowly job of burning the shitters.

Even though Union II would begin May 26, 1967, Fox Company of the 2nd Battalion, 5th Marine Regiment, 1st Marine Division would be held in reserve, until May 30. At this time 2/5 would be heli-lifted out to the Operational areas of 1st and 3rd Battalion of the 5th Marine Regiment, (1/5 and 3/5), of the 1st Marine Division.

Author holding his M-16 in a bunker on Phu Lac 6, a few miles from An Hoa. This area contained many mines and booby traps. This was the proximity where a Viet Cong sniper shot him with a Thompson Sub Machine Gun.

Author with his M-60 machine gun in the battalion area of An Hoa.

Blasen shaving in the battalion area of An Hoa. He would be KIA on June 2 on Operation Union II.

Operation Union II Unit Coordination

Union II, as in Union, involved coordination between the 6th ARVN Regiment and the 1st ARVN Ranger Group. The 1st and 3rd Battalions of the 5th Marines would once again act as maneuver elements for III MAF. The main blocking unit would be Hilgartner's 1_{st} Battalion, setting up in the western portion of the Que Son Basin. At the same time, three Republic of Vietnam (RVN) Ranger Group Battalions would be attacking southwest from Thang Binh and two battalions of the 6th ARVN Regiment, would launch an attack northwest from Tam Ky. Esslinger's 3rd Battalion would chopper into the south end of the basin and sweep towards the northeast. Code name for the ARVN's portion of the operation is Lien Kit 106.

The 2nd NVA Division was commanded by Major General Hoang Thoa and his superior, Major General Dan Quang Trung, who was able to supply him with an additional one thousand fresh troops from North Vietnam via the Ho Chi Minh Trail, also known as the Truong Son Trail, near the Que Son Basin.

May 26 - Meeting the Enemy Head-on

Five kilometers east of Nui Loc Son Outpost, Esslinger's three Marine companies, India, Lima & Mike, of 3/5 and a command group, made a heli-borne assault on the morning of May 26. Only sporadic sniper fire greeted Lima Company's first two waves putting down at Landing Zone (LZ), code name Eagle. Mike Company and the command group experienced a completely different situation as stiff small arms and mortar fire saturated the LZ with one CH-46 helicopter being shot down.

Lima and Mike Companies attacked north to relieve pressure on the LZ as India Company was landing. The two attacking companies found well entrenched enemy positions northeast of the LZ. While the enemy positions were being hammered by artillery and air strikes, India Company outflanked the enemy's front lines and under intense opposition, drove through their entrenched positions. Prior to over running the positions, the Marines had taken many casualties from the heavy automatic weapons and mortar fire.

The Marines, under the command of Lieutenant Colonel Esslinger, exacted an even heavier toll. Enemy positions throughout the battlefield, continually gave up corpses and wounded. The count totaled 118 dead, while U.S. forces suffered thirty-eight killed and eighty-two wounded, including Lieutenant Colonel Esslinger. Lieutenant Colonel Webster would assume command of 3/5.

While 3/5 occupied the NVA's attention, other units were positioning themselves as a blocking force to the northwest. ARVN forces in the meantime, were working their way in from the northeast and the southeast in an attempt to box in the enemy force.

For the next three days, units sweeping through the area, encountered only sporadic sniper fire. Thinking the 2nd NVA Division had again eluded them and abandoned the basin, the South Vietnamese closed down their portion of the operation, known as Lien Kit 106.

Colonel Houghton thought otherwise. He had a gut feeling that they had merely moved to another part of the basin and began making plans accordingly.

May 30 - Fox Company Mobilizes

Houghton's re-examination of the existing intelligence prompted a new attack strategy in the basin. His units would push to the hills along the rim of the corridor southeast of 3rd Battalion's May 26 engagement. On this day his two battalions were flown to the area and began sweeping to the northeast. Only long range sniper fire was encountered.

While Houghton's battalions were sweeping northeast, the reserve forces of 2nd Battalion, 5th Marines were boarding Sea Knight helicopters at the battalion area of An Hoa. There was a mound of green left on the tarmac after the sea knights had departed. A decision had been made by Captain Graham to leave our flak jackets behind. They were just too hot and cumbersome and slowed us down when we needed to make a hurried advance to the battle area. I do believe he made the right decision. 2/5 was heading to the Tam Ky area to set up a blocking force near the entrance of the basin; thus attempting to trap enemy units the ARVN forces had been pursuing for the past several days.

The choppers stayed in loose formation, until they began their descent to the LZ, which is northeast of the May 26 battle site. The plan was for 2/5 to begin their sweep in a southwesterly direction.

My gun team was selected as part of the LZ securing party. The adrenaline is racing when approaching an unsecured LZ in a slow moving chopper. You continually ask yourself, "Is it hot or is it cold?" After departing the CH-46 A Sea Knights, we set up in what was considered a cold landing zone. Almost immediately, listening posts were sent out to keep tabs on any enemy movement in the area.

It took some time for the rest of the battalion to land and regroup. With the last of the choppers arriving, a platoon of Fox Company took the point and headed into the valley. Helicopter gun ships were constantly reconnoitering our advance since we were now out of range of any artillery support.

My gun team was assigned to 2nd platoon, who with 1st Platoon, was called on to silence rifle fire coming from a grassy knoll. We assaulted the small hill without taking any casualties. We set up a perimeter and stayed till morning.

May 31 - Snipers are neutralized

We found ourselves up and moving off the hill even before the sun had a chance to make its appearance. We joined with the rest of the company in the valley, and after acquiring our day's water supply, we moved across the valley to the base of a large hill. We immediately came under sniper fire. My gunner set in and began hammering the hillside with rhythmic fire, when his gun suddenly went quiet and yelled that he couldn't see. A near miss had scattered dirt up into his eyes, and while tending to him another incoming round hit my pack, penetrating, but causing no physical damage. Fire superiority was finally regained and the hill was taken.

First and second platoons began digging in while a squad size patrol was sent out in pursuit of the snipers. The patrol soon returned, bearing a Browning Automatic Rifle and two VC prisoners. The patrol had surprised the three man gun team, killing one and wounding the other two.

We did our best to get some sleep. Being under constant fire while assaulting these hills, was taking its toll. A few more days and Union II would be history.

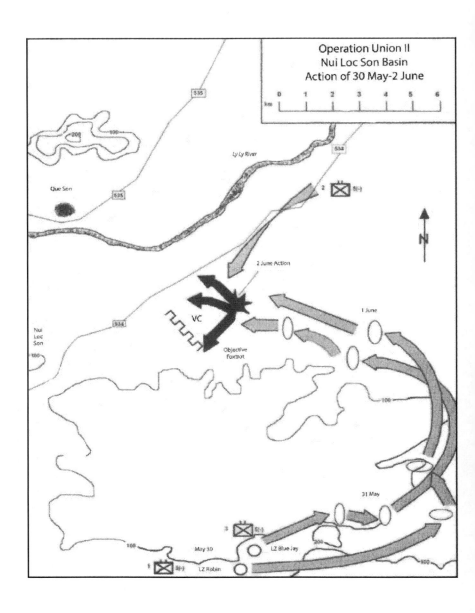

June 1 - The Calm before the Storm

This morning we continued on up the valley and made contact with a few residents from the local village. Their village was quite small, but seemed to hold an excessive amount of rice and other food stuffs. They were very fearful on our approach and cowered under our questioning, but refused to divulge any helpful information. These villagers were caught in the middle, with us on one side and the Viet Cong on the other. If they aided us in any way, the Viet Cong would eventually find a way to make them pay. Because they appeared so uneasy, it prompted us to be even more cautious; so much so that we had the head chieftain and a few others helicoptered out for questioning.

We continued our push down the ever narrowing valley until our point man called a halt. He had come upon a large tunnel complex with tear gas emanating from one of the entrance holes. The tunnels were searched, and after determining they were empty, were destroyed using demolitions. C-4, a pliable plastic explosive with a delayed fuse, was used to blow the complex. The delay would give us time to leave the area, knowing full well that the sound of the explosion would draw in unwanted guests. We dug in early this day to prepare for incoming resupply choppers, carrying rations, ammo and explosives.

So far, the large enemy force we had been pursuing had not materialized and with only a couple of operational days left, the chance of contact seemed minimal. The end of Union II would place us in close proximity to where the operation had its beginning. Tomorrow would end the more strenuous portions of Union II, if contact wasn't made.

June 2 - Fox Company Steps into Hell

This day found the 1st and 3rd Battalions moving abreast from the southeast towards the northwest, while the reserve units of 2nd Battalion, 5th Marines were coming in from the northeast and heading in a southwesterly direction. Foxtrot was moving between two boulder strewn and brush choked hills, designated, A and B which funneled into a large rice paddy. The other side of the rice paddy was Foxtrot's objective, Vinh Huy 2, a partially destroyed French ville.

At approximately 0930, two companies of the 3rd Battalion were subjected to intense fire from about 200 dug-in troops of NVA. We were a mere 1000 meters from our objective and only 3000 meters from the May 26 engagement.

2nd Platoon of Fox 2/5 also made contact with a smaller enemy force as they negotiated a boulder strewn hill of about forty meters in height. Contact was made when one of Corporal Ted Verena's riflemen, Lance Corporal Daniel Yeutter, left the group to investigate a pile of rocks. A burst of AK-47 rifle fire filled the air. The Marine had been hit at point blank range and suffered severe sucking chest wounds. Even though severely wounded, he was able to tell us that the enemy troops were not Viet Cong, but instead hard-core or North Vietnamese Regulars. While Corporal Barnes worked on Yuetter's chest wounds, 1st squad and my gun team, immediately set up a perimeter, with my gun covering the paddy to the north and west.

It wasn't long before we noticed movement along the edge of the rice paddy, and while spotting for my gunner, began shooting. I picked up an NVA moving from right to left in my sights and pulled. Since I was shooting tracers, it wasn't too difficult to see the rounds piercing his body. My gunner and the rest of the platoon were also in on the action and it wasn't long before all enemy soldiers were down.

We moved off the hill and into the paddy to search the downed soldiers. The NVA, in their khaki uniforms, were heavily laden with full packs, Rocket Propelled Grenades (RPGs), AK-47s and rounds for heavy mortars. They seemed to be well nourished, clean and so very, very young. After the dead and wounded were searched and the prisoners secured, we continued our advance into the paddy.

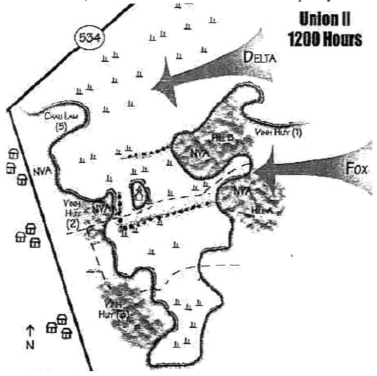

Courtesy, Lieutenant Colonel David B. Brown, (Retired)

3rd Battalion remained engaged in savage fighting, but by 1300 hours was able to overrun the enemy positions with help from supporting arms. "Casualties were being evacuated when a medevac took a direct hit from a 57mm recoiless rifle, killing one Marine and wounding seven others."

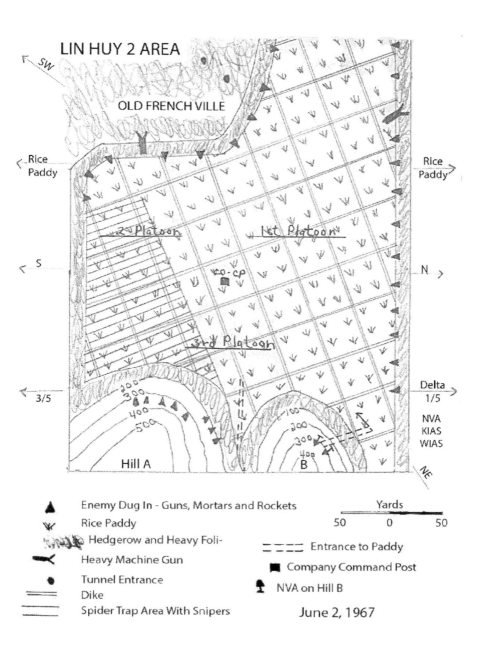

While 3rd Battalion, now under the command of Lieutenant Colonel Webster, remained in contact with the enemy, Hilgartner's 1st Battalion moved to his aid. The frontal assault consisted of Delta Company 1/5 on the right and 1st and 2nd platoons of Fox 2/5 on the left with 3rd platoon of Foxtrot slightly to the rear. In command was Captain Graham with Headquarters, whose position was near our company's center. The assault units moved down into the 1000 meter wide rice paddy with a horseshoe shaped tree line surrounding it on three sides. The hedgerows could only be reached by crossing the dry open paddy. The fortified positions of the NVA opened up with devastating fire from the hedgerow, hitting first the left flank and then sweeping through to the middle of the frontal assault. I believe this is when 2nd Lieutenant Straughan Kelsey from 2nd platoon was killed. He was hit just after his M-16 had jammed as did many others that day. Ever since we were issued this weapon, we have had problems and I spent a lot of time running around unjamming these rifles with my cleaning rod. I had come across a hand written note, during my research, from a high ranking Marine officer that stated that this was the worst weapon ever issued to an American soldier. To state such an opinion at the time was political suicide. The 3rd Platoon tried in vain to outflank the NVA positions, but were forced back by the intense automatic weapons fire.

My gun team, under the leadership of Corporal Barnes, was assigned to 2nd Platoon and Headquarters. While 1st and 2nd Platoons were fighting on Delta 1/5's left, all hell broke loose. The crossfire was so intense it seemed as though a wall of lead was blocking our advance. We continued at a fast pace towards our objective, firing our weapons in an attempt to regain fire superiority.

My gun position was now near the front of 2nd Platoon flanked by riflemen on either side. I looked left and saw Corporal Westphal in a typical 'John Wayne Assault' moving towards the tree line. After checking my right flank, I glanced again at Westphal, but this time he was down. The devastating fire was opening large holes in the assault line with dead and wounded lying everywhere. The assault had stalled in the middle of the paddy. Machine gun and automatic rifle fire continued as a barrage of 81/82mm mortars began walking through our ranks. Strikes from fixed wing and artillery began hitting the bunker complex in the tree line. Alpha 1/5 had made it to the rice paddy to the left of Foxtrot, but was also stalled by the intense fire coming from the tree line and paddy area.

Jets Hit Enemy Positions

Marines carry a wounded Leatherneck for medical evacuation during Operation Union II, north of Chu Lai. Phantom jets of Marine Fighter Attack Squadron-542 hit a fortified enemy treeline position, smoking in the background. (Photo By: Sgt. Gary Thomas)

I was visually combing the area in front of me, when I noticed some slight movement coming from Westphal. At this point, I also noticed that not all the rifle fire was coming from the hedgerow, but was coming from a closer proximity where we were stalled. I realized that snipers lay in spider traps scattered throughout the paddy area. We were being held down by the weapons fire from the hedgerow while the snipers were picking us off one at a time. A round from one of these spider traps may have been responsible for Westphal's injuries. The traps were hidden under rice fodder and very nearly overlooked had it not been for a sharp-eyed and experienced Kit Carson Scout, Kinh, who had been assigned to Staff Sergeant Anthony Morengo's unit. (All Kit Carson Scouts were former Viet Cong.) The scout and several riflemen were taking them out, one by one, until thirty-one of the enemy lay dead.

An opportunity presented itself during the air-strikes for a rescue attempt for Westphal. I related my decision to go after Westphal to Corporal Barnes, and he immediately said no. He stated that he would go instead, at which time I emphatically disagreed. I said matter-of-factly that I was not married and that he was, at which point I took off.

It took only seconds to cover the fifteen or so meters to where the Marine lay. I quickly got in behind and grabbed him around his chest for the drag back. I decided to catch my breath first, which proved to be a mistake. The time it took me to catch my breath was also enough time to question what I was doing there in the open rice paddy. I had left the relative safety of a paddy dike to rescue a wounded Marine, in an open hostile environment full of flying lead. The fear that gripped me held me completely immobile, until Barnes' voice jarred me back to reality. He had followed me in and I can remember him saying, "John, I'll help ya," He grabbed Westphal and we proceeded to carry him back to the protection of the dike. He was unconscious, but breathing. It was but a moment before his body shuddered and his final breath left his lungs. He had died from a severe head wound. A bullet had entered his brain through the left side of his face. It was a miracle he lived as long as he had and most probably died a painless death. Even in death he appeared passive and relaxed, with a slight smile etched into his face. That moment will remain with me forever.

We were taking fire from the front and the two flanks when all of a sudden we were taking automatic weapons fire from the hill overlooking the rice paddy to our rear. This is when 3rd platoon went into action. Corporal Perry Jones' gun team was involved in flushing out the enemy and silencing the guns. They maneuvered up the face while others out flanked the enemy by taking the high ground. The hostile fire was neutralized and some pressure was taken off of 1st and 2nd platoons.

Corporal Pat "Water Bu" Haley, a rocket squad leader, was also with 3rd platoon, but found himself armed only with a 45 caliber hand gun. Not too good when you're up against machine guns and automatic rifles.

Another hero of the day was Corporal Melvin M. Long. He was involved in taking out the gun emplacements on Hill A that were causing such havoc on 1st and 2nd platoons. He had made his way up the back side of hill A and eventually took up a position above the enemy where he could direct fire into their reinforced trench line. He was standing on an out cropping, completely exposed, firing and changing magazines as needed. Even after being wounded, he continued his assault until the hostile fire ceased. Six NVA bodies were pulled from the trench line.

Another Marine to be mentioned here is Private First Class Melvin Earl Newlin. He was able to survive Union II only to be killed July 4 at Nong Son, the coal mine fourteen miles west of An Hoa. Due to his actions, he received the Medal of Honor.

June 2 - The Annihilation of 2nd Platoon

The 2nd Platoon, under Captain Graham's command, had been hit the hardest and was still being hammered by two machine gun positions sweeping the paddy. We were up against Major Dao Cong's 2nd Battalion, 31st NVA regiment, who had hammered the hell out of Delta just a short time ago. Orders came down to take the tree line and knock out the guns.

Controversy still clouds this particular time period. It was said by those near the Captain, that he had tried at least three times to continue the fixed wing strikes to the paddy and into the hedgerow. He related our predicament to the higher echelon that we either get continued air support or withdraw from the immediate area as the odds of reaching the hedgerow as an intact force were not in our favor. His request was denied and further orders would be strictly adhered to. The orders stood: secure the hedgerow and take out the gun bunkers. To this day anger still seethes with some of the noncoms who were stranded out in the rice paddy. Remarks were recorded in the 2/5 After Action Report for Union II, stating that closer coordination between air and ground forces had to be maintained. Further study would be forthcoming.

It was at this time that Captain Graham moved up and through 2nd Platoon with his Headquarters Group, taking along several of us still able to fight. I told my gunner Private First Class Robert Mills, to wait in the paddy for ammo resupply before advancing to the tree line. Corporal Rick Barnes, myself and two other riflemen were at the farthest point in the assault line and would be the first to reach our objectives. When we got the order to move, we came up out of the paddy like screaming banshees. Captain Graham, Corporal Barnes and several marines from Headquarters, went through an opening to the left and took out several crew served weapons, including one of the machine guns. I entered through the right, just behind another Marine who immediately dropped from a grazing head wound. Another rifleman followed in behind me and he too, was instantly hit by the same sniper. I was cussing to high heaven trying to find that bastard, firing into every likely spot that could be concealing him. My attention was riveted to a bamboo root system into which I fired my remaining rounds. Whether I took him out, I don't know, but the sniping ceased.

Corporal Barnes said that the screaming assault so unnerved the enemy that they streamed from their entrenched positions leaving several crew served weapons intact, including one of the machine guns, which was immediately dismantled.

I moved about fifty meters further back into the undergrowth to clear out any snipers who might still be lurking near our newly secured perimeter. There were fresh fighting holes and tunnel entrances everywhere. I began depositing my remaining grenades. At that point, I was weaponless except for my physical abilities in hand to hand combat and the thought was anything but comforting. Movement to my left front stopped me dead in my tracks. At first I only saw bushes, but on closer examination the bushes became two perfectly camouflaged NVA soldiers. They were within twenty-five meters of me and both carried AK-47 assault rifles. We stood transfixed with each other, neither of us daring to move a muscle. Knowing my own predicament, I thought that anytime now I would be taking in rounds. To my surprise the two NVA disappeared silently into the foliage and suddenly everything became deathly quiet. I returned to the tree line and found the rest of 2nd Platoon and Headquarters Group inside the hedgerow setting up a temporary defensive perimeter. We were tired, thirsty and out of ammo and basically thought the battle was over.

It was near 1415 and our units had been in hostile contact with the 2nd NVA Division since 0930 that morning. We were now set up in the ruins of an old French Villa, Vinh Huy 2, with some of the old stucco walls still standing. I found some stagnant water in an old concrete pot, which I shared with several of the others. It was hot, filthy stuff, but it still tasted good. We relaxed while the rest of the company made their way towards our position.

Marines from the 2nd Battalion, 5th Marines, exit helicopters in a hot landing zone on their way to reinforce fellow Marines in June 1967, USMC

Refer to page 112 for further information on above photo.

June 2 - Surviving the Counter Attack

I was sitting with two other riflemen on an old house bunker, not too far from where Corporal Barnes was resting.

Captain Graham was just inside the tree line in radio contact with his CO. His radioman was by his side.

The explosion was deafening. I found myself lying prone some distance from where I'd been sitting only seconds before. My rifle had been literally torn from my hands and this loud ringing filled the inside of my head. I had felt my face being ripped apart and foreign particles entering my body from head to toe. The red hot metal buried deeply into my flesh without any noticeable pain present. Besides the shrapnel, the concussion from the blast wreaked havoc with my thigh muscles, mincing them up like ground hamburger.

I managed to get up on my hands and knees and slowly lifted my head to scan the surroundings. Marines were moving past me through a thick cloud of dust and debris and everything seemed to be in slow motion, almost as if you were in a drug-induced world. I noticed one of the Marines, Corporal O'Brien, staring wide-eyed at me and yelling, "Corpsman up, Gobrecht's hit bad." Even though I was severely wounded, I was still mobile enough to evade the mortar barrage hitting our position. Finally, I found shelter against one of the stucco ruins, along with Barnes and O'Brien, who were also hit. Nearly everyone was dead or wounded and the thought of capture and complete annihilation was very real.

Captain Graham was about where I had last seen him and slightly wounded. He opted to stay with his radioman (Corporal Marion Lee Dirickson) who was also down and unable to move. Word came over the radio that Sergeant Ackley was dead from chest wounds. By this time Doc Donovan had made it up to check on the more severely wounded, although little good came of it, since he had long since used up his precious morphine and other medical supplies.

My injuries were such that I didn't think my chance of survival was very high and decided to release my diary to Doc's care. My simple instructions were, "Just send it home to my family." At all costs, I needed to keep it out of enemy hands.

Captain Graham was in direct communications with a fixed wing pilot. The fighter pilot asked Captain Graham three times to confirm the order to drop the ordinance directly on top of our position. On confirmation he went into a wide sweeping arc, preparing to come in for the bomb drop. The fly boys had confirmed the presence of a large enemy force moving towards our position and advised all those able, to move into the paddy. The Captain relayed the message to us and stated that as of this moment we were on our own. He ordered Gunny Green and all those able, back across the paddy to where 3rd Platoon had set up. One of these was Private First Class Tom Labarbera and was the last of that group to talk to Captain Graham. I think he thought at the time, that everyone but Captain Graham and his radioman Dirickson were the only two remaining behind. In fact there were three more of us, wounded so badly that we needed to stay near the Captain. Doc Donovan also made the decision to remain with us, despite his wounds, to care for our wounds. It wasn't until a unit reunion in D.C. that Labarbera heard from Barnes and me the rest of the story.

Captain Graham said to the remaining five of us to pull ourselves together and fight with every means available to thwart capture and torture or possible execution. The Captain ordered all those able, to move into the rice paddy, because of imminent air strikes being directed to coordinates at our present location. Everyone knew by the sound of rifle fire that the NVA were closing in.

Corporal Barnes took a quick look behind the ruins and saw the khaki-uniformed NVA bearing down on our position and told O'Brien and me that "we have to get the hell out of here." Corporal Barnes saw how badly my thigh had been shredded and asked if I thought I could make it? I said, "I think I can." He said, "When you hit the paddy, John, you go to the left, O'Brien, you hit the middle and I'll move to the right. That way one round won't take out all three of us at once." It was agreed to and we executed.

The lapse of time at the wall had drained me of additional blood and strength. I felt so very weak. The left side of my body was now wracked with pain and I was stiffening up terribly. Once up we made our way to the paddy. We went maybe thirty meters into the paddy, under intense fire, before dropping in behind a foot high rice dike. Barnes and I made it, but O'Brien was dead. O'Brien had been on the ground only seconds before Doc was at his side. Doc never knew what hit him. As close as Doc had been to O'Brien, the NVA had been to Doc and instantly directed a bullet into Doc's skull.

Corporal Barnes was watching the entire picture unfold in front of him and knew that either he or I would be next. He had a grenade on his belt, but because of excessive damage to his arms, couldn't get to it to pull the pin. I was lying on my back and really couldn't see what was going on, and at that point, didn't really care.

The NVA who had shot Donovan was now standing next to Barnes and gave him a kick to see if he was dead. Barnes was playing dead as was I, and never moved; the blood pulsating from his wrist seemed to authenticate it. Thinking Barnes dead, his attention was focused on me. Was I worth wasting a bullet on or not? He never had time to decide one way or the other, for at that very instant the air strikes came screaming in.

All of a sudden the ground shook as a jet streaked in from the blue, strafing the area with 20mm cannon rounds. The strafing had the enemy running for the safety of their tunnels. The jets came in low and hard, dropping their payload of 250 and 500 pound bombs. The entire tree line was exploding in flame and our concern was being charred by our own arsenal. We were no more than forty or fifty meters from the impact area and metal shards began singing over the foot high dike.

During the short lull in the bombing, Corporal Barnes yelled over and asked how I was doing? In response I gave a thumbs up. He then suggested that we wait till dusk and begin crawling slightly away from each other, to make it more difficult for the enemy to follow our blood trails. That was the last contact I had with him, until he phoned twenty-four years later.

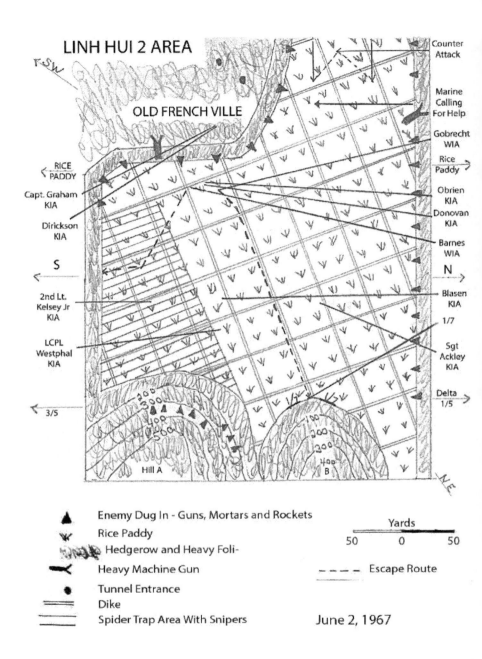

We met in 2008 at a unit reunion, where he told me what transpired during his escape. Day was turning to night and as he was crawling at an angle towards the tree line to his right, he noticed movement. At first he couldn't quite make it out, but as he focused, it seemed as if someone was waving to get his attention. It slightly unnerved him because NVA and VC had been filtering into the paddy looking for their own dead and wounded.

Finally it occurred to him that there were marines in the tree line and wanted him to crawl over to where they were. Now he thought, "Why don't they come and get me? I'm the one wounded." Anyway it turned out to be Gunny Green and several others and they were able to get Corporal Barnes out early that evening. He was put on a medevac and flown to Chu Lai.

Word was now beginning to filter back to An Hoa that Foxtrot 2/5 was in a lot of trouble and fighting for its survival. When Hotel 2/5 heard about foxtrot's plight they were livid and couldn't understand why they weren't aboard choppers heading into the melee. We were sister companies and had fought together in Operation Tuscaloosa. Captain Graham was with Hotel at the time, but shortly thereafter transferred to Foxtrot. After a few hours they were finally loading up the choppers, but yet no word was given to execute and just idled there on the tarmac. More time passed and the word came to stand down. The reserve unit was no longer needed. Captain Graham was dead as was most of 2nd Platoon with 1st Platoon also suffering heavy casualties. 1/7 had arrived from Hill 55 and was able to take some pressure off of Foxtrot. Through his actions, Captain Graham would posthumously receive the Medal of Honor.

Near nightfall, Corporal Barnes made contact with Marines working their way toward our position using the hedgerow as cover. His legs weren't injured and he was able to make steady progress to their location. I was in really bad shape and moved a lot more slowly in between the air strikes. I spoke to one Marine, Gunny Green, at a unit reunion, who had been involved in the rescue attempt. He said that they were within thirty meters of my position before being forced back.

Word was passed on to battalion that 2nd Platoon, as a unit, ceased to exist. Perry Jones, team leader from 3rd Platoon, had witnessed O'Brien being shot down. Perry and the rest of the platoon were dug in on the one hill overlooking the paddy and hedgerow where they visually witnessed our destruction. He said he felt anger, but at the same time felt like crying.

At about the same time Corporal Barnes and I were fighting for our survival, Captain Graham had been fighting for his life. Even though he had ordered us into the paddy, he remained in the tree line to protect the injured radioman and our retreat. His last radio transmission was that he was being assaulted by a force of twenty-five enemy soldiers. He died protecting his injured radioman and the two of us left in the rice paddy, a mere forty meters from his desperate stand. When the NVA began closing on our position, we knew Captain Graham was dead.

By nightfall the reserve companies had yet to arrive and Lieutenant Colonel Jackson, because of the urgency of the situation, requested to attack without them. The request was granted.

They hadn't gone far into the darkness, when they slammed into a large NVA force trying to flee towards the north. The Marines quickly drove through the enemy force and began moving to the south. In the meantime, the NVA force seeing its exit blocked began withdrawing to the southwest.

I was content to lie right where I was, up until I began hearing movement out in the paddy. The voices were Vietnamese. Enemy troops were beginning their infiltration back into the paddy area searching for wounded and any equipment left behind. Any wounded Marines found would probably be shot. They tried mimicking a Marine patrol, out to aid any wounded left behind during the heat of battle. Their heavily accented, broken English, gave away their identity. I know from experience that being alone on a battlefield is scary as hell. We were left there because of our wounds and sacrificed as individuals so the entire unit wouldn't be lost. I knew that when the chance did arise, a rescue effort would be forthcoming. Time was fast running out for some of us. I was able to keep a relatively cool head, not because I was one brave Marine, but because I was scared to death of possible capture. It was capture, not death, that terrified me. There was one Marine who wasn't faring so well. When the NVA were searching and calling, he was answering. The only advantage to this situation was the fact that he was drawing them away from me.

From the sound of his location, I would say he was from Delta Company. I could follow the progress of the NVA by sound and could hear the Marine answering, "Oh God, help me, please help me!" over and over again. I kept telling him, in whispered tones, to just shut the hell up, damn it, keep quiet. His yelling was cut short by a single gunshot and I knew it was time for me to move.

June 2 - Night Escape

I tried pulling myself along, with my right arm pulling and my right leg pushing, but the expenditure of energy moved me only inches. The NVA were somewhere to my rear and would eventually find me, unless I found a faster way out. I either had to walk out or lie where I was and hope they would pass by. I decided to try and walk.

The worst part was getting up and balancing all my weight on my right side. My left appendages hurt like hell and were stiff as wood. I was able to move maybe five feet before toppling over. I'd lay there, totally resigned to the fact I wasn't going to make it, until I'd hear the broken English, which would again jump start me into renewing my effort. This was a continuing cycle for the next few hours. I only advanced under total darkness and remained motionless when the falling flares lit up the night sky.

While making my way through the darkness, reinforcements of the 7th Marines were landing in a distant LZ and racing to our position. On board was one Gordon Fowler, a United States Marine Corps Combat Correspondent of I Corp. Before his involvement in Union II, he had been out with Reconnaissance (Recon) and a few patrols with the 7th Marines, but never involved in anything considered as dangerous combat, until that day in June, when he boarded a chopper for the Que Son Valley. Fowler came up with descriptions of the Que Son Battle as such: "They (the 5th Marines) had a division on them and were getting cut up. The valley was completely lit up and the horizon was glowing. There were flare-ships up, gun ships shooting, and air strikes going in. It looked like something out of the apocalypse. I had been in mortar attacks, but this was incredible. We were just absolutely bracketed."

The gunships I am referring to were AC-47 cargo aircraft fitted with gatling guns. Nicknames for the ships were Spooky, Puff the Magic Dragon and Dragonships. They could fire 6,000 rounds a minute and cover every square yard of a football field in three seconds. The solid ribbon of tracer rounds reminded a person of a dragon spitting flame from its huge mouth.

My progress through the night was slow, but steady. My main purpose was to locate a friendly force, but I had no idea of where to look. All I knew was that I was moving in the opposite direction of where the battle had taken place. I had already been moving several hours through the darkness, when I discerned movement and heard voices up ahead. I froze as a flare burst overhead, illuminating the paddy around me. Ahead were Marines making their way back as I was. Most were wounded and the least serious were carrying out the more seriously hurt.

Bodies littered the artificially lit fields, looking more like hell than earth. Satan had done his job well. Marines and NVA alike lay alone or together on intertwined piles. This was a nightmare come true.

No one would give me any water, because of the nature of my wounds. They weren't sure if any of the metal shards had penetrated into my intestinal area and drinking water with that condition could kill me.

I continued on with the rest of the wounded, most of whom were from Delta 1/5. Going only a short distance further, I was brought up short by a wounded Marine, lying against the dike. He was a rifleman from Fox Company and couldn't move his legs. He was near panic and held me at gunpoint saying I wasn't going anywhere without him. He was just so damn scared. I made my way over to him and told him I'd do whatever I could to help him. Moving him even a short distance proved impossible, so I did the next best thing. Combining our efforts, he was able to move far enough to get protection in behind a dead Marine. I helped him prop up his rifle and scrounged around for additional ammo. I promised to send help as soon as I made it back, and I thought to myself, "If I make it back." Before leaving, I reassured him that I wouldn't let him down. He was resting comfortably upon my departure and I now had real purpose to keep going. The decision to leave him haunts me still. If it had been my brother, would I have made the same decision? I hope so, but I can't say positively that I would have.

I continued on, with flares bursting constantly overhead. The main fighting seemed to be off in the distance of maybe a mile or so, although spurts of automatic weapons fire and mortar attacks continued around us. Moving parallel to the dike, a Marine yelled over to me that Lance Corporal Blasen had been found. His body lay next to another dike where he had succumbed to a head wound. The war had taken a horrendous toll of the young.

June 3 - The Ups and Downs of Rescue

It was probably early morning and flares were still dropping constantly. As the light from one of these flares flooded the landscape, I spotted Marines along the base of a small hill to my front. This was probably a unit from 1st Battalion, 7th Marine Regiment (1/7). It seemed to take forever to cover the short distance to the newly secured area. Once there, the adrenaline surge was gone and with it my strength. I collapsed. It was as if I were an actor in an old time western, where the wounded cowboy rides to town for help and once there falls from his horse, says a few words and passes out.

I communicated directly to the first Marine I came in contact with, that there was a rifleman and scores of other dead and wounded in need of immediate help along the dike I had just followed in. I also related that many NVA were out and about. A patrol was immediately dispatched and hopefully rescue for the helpless was imminent. A poncho would act as a litter and I was carried to the top of the hill to an LZ.

1/7 and most likely 3rd Platoon of 2/5 were having trouble with this hill as automatic weapons fire and mortars kept hitting inside the perimeter. There was also talk of NVA using flame throwers (this could have been misleading information) to probe the Marine perimeter.

The action going on around me meant little. All I desired now more than anything was a drink of water. I felt like a wounded animal wanting only to be near a cool stream to rest and lick my wounds. I felt myself slipping into a delirium state for lack of precious bodily fluids. My inner self was on fire and my brain no longer registered rational thoughts. Control over my speech was gone and the rhythmic sound, "Water, water, water" was spilling from me.

A Second Lieutenant came to me and with much patience and sympathy, told me why he couldn't give me anything to drink. He departed and I helplessly returned to my rhythmic chant. The officer returned and laid a wet cloth over my cracked, dry lips. The moisture did little to quench my need for water, but it did feel cool and uplifting.

I must have been near where 3rd Platoon of 2/5 was set in, because I found out years later that Dean Johnson had seen me just before I was loaded on the medevac. Johnson and I had been together since boot camp, and had even entered the Marine Corp on the buddy system. Even though I was delirious, I did remember him being there.

A passing CH-53 Sikorsky was called in by the Battalion's forward observer to aid in the evacuation of the more seriously wounded. Litters of dead and wounded were loaded aboard and finally I was laid just inside the rear loading ramp. I thought to myself, "I'm safe and on my way home." Just after the ramp locked shut we came under intense mortar and small arms fire. The chopper managed to get airborne even after taking multiple hits from a mortar and small arms.

I lost track of time and didn't know if we'd been aloft a few minutes or an hour when the alert was sounded, "Mayday, Mayday" and knew we were going down. The pilot was in radio contact with Da Nang Air Field and relayed that we had been hit and were going to crash. Since there was ample time to give coordinates, I believe that the damage sustained was hydraulic or in the fuel lines. When we did hit, I merely felt a sudden jolt and was unconscious until being carried through the double doors of the hospital.

I also remember the doctor looking down at me with a grin on his face as I tried smiling back. He said I was safe now and they would do everything possible to save my leg. I'm sure my thigh looked worse than it really was, from all the debris ground into the wounds. I was just glad to be alive and began my drift into dreamland.

Through research and my own experience, I am able to give some details of the medevac crash. During a phone conversation with Corporal Barnes, he was able to fill me in on additional details taking place after the crash. He said that during the early morning hours of June 3, they brought in a medevac pilot and placed him in the bed next to him. He told Rick that a unit involved in Operation Union II radioed him to aid in the evacuation of dead and wounded from the previous day's fighting. He had gone into the LZ and on taking off had taken quite a few hits. The chopper stayed aloft all the way to Da Nang before going down.

The crash had been worse than I initially thought. The pilot related to Corporal Barnes that only two others on board had survived the crash; one other Marine and me. The rest perished, either from the mortar or rifle fire or from the crash itself. I must have been knocked unconscious for an unknown period of time. At Da Nang the ground crews reported back to 2nd Battalion that fifty-eight holes were found in the CH-53 medevac.

The sudden appearance of Marines on the NVA's northern flank hastened the enemy's disengagement and eventual retreat to the southwest. Once in the open, Phantom 104 jet (F-4) air strikes devastated the enemy's ranks. The 5th Marines spent the remainder of the night regrouping their units and evacuating casualties.

The next morning all three battalions swept the battlefield and counted 476 dead NVA in and around the contested paddy and hedgerow complex. We also suffered heavily with seventy-one Marines killed and another 139 wounded. Many Marines attached to Fox Company were also killed and wounded. This is when my diary was found on Doc Donovan's body.

During the sweep Colonel Hilgartner received a radio message that NVA troops were also out collecting their dead and wounded. An undeclared truce remained in effect the rest of the day with no shots being fired by either side. This gave the Colonel his chance to recover Captain Graham's body and any other Marines left behind in the heat of battle. This is when my machine gunner, Private First Class Robert Mills, was found hiding in some boulders not too far from where I had left him in the paddy to await ammo resupply.

It was noted years later, from a Marine participating in the June 3 sweep, that the Captain had died where I last saw him, near the edge of the hedgerow. He lay as if he were on a movie set in some John Wayne war movie. He was in a natural prone position when found. There were three radios captured by the enemy, and no doubt, one came from the radioman Captain Graham was trying to protect. There must have been only enough time for the NVA to strip off the radio before the air strikes began hitting the tree line. In most incidences the Captain would have been dragged away and/or his body mutilated. The worst thing imaginable was being an MIA.

Enemy troops withdrew carrying their wounded on a travois, an apparatus using two poles lashed together similar to what the nomadic plains Indians of our own west used to transport their belongings. The day after the undeclared truce, Marine units tried following the travois skid marks of the 2nd NVA Division, but to no avail. Helicopters constantly being called in to evacuate the wounded, caused by the enemy's rear guard, slowed down the units in pursuit. The main force eventually escaped.

The heavy June 2 fighting was the last significant engagement of Union II. Total enemy casualties were 701 killed with twenty-three others captured. Marines also suffered heavily with 110 killed, same as in Union 1, and 241 wounded. It must also be remembered that Union II was of much shorter duration than Union 1 and most of the casualties resulted from the May 26 and June 2 battles. The June 2 encounter with the 2nd NVA Division, will go down as the most intense fighting for the 5th Marines since their arrival in South Vietnam, in April of 1966.

Fox Company 2/5 would continue to be placed in areas of high intense enemy concentrations and heavy fighting would continue. One such place was Nong Son, South Vietnam's only active coal mine and a place where an eighteen year old machine-gunner, Private Melvin Newlin from Fox 2/5 would posthumously be awarded the Medal of Honor. Later the 5th Marines, including other Marine units would fight for twenty-six days, against 12,000 crack NVA troops in and around the Imperial City of Hue. It would mark, for all practical purposes, the end of the Viet Cong political structure and the dominance of the North Vietnamese over all Vietnamese.

Although enemy forces suffered heavily during the two Union Operations, they repeatedly pumped in replacements in their attempt to regain control of the Que Son Region.

Area Marine Is Wounded Second Time

Combat wounds have hospitalized a Hanover area Marine for the second time within six weeks in South Vietnam. Marine Lance Corporal John W. Gobrecht, son of Mr. and Mrs. William H. Gobrecht, Fairview Dr., Hanover R. D. 1, was hit by shrapnel during an operation in the Quang Nam region last Saturday, according to word received by the parents.

Corporal Gobrecht suffered extensive wounds on the left side from his face to his feet when a shell exploded near him, his parents were informed by two Marine officers from Columbia during a visit to the Gobrecht home last night.

The wounded Corporal was admitted for treatment at the First Medical Battalion Unit at Da Nang where his condition was listed as "good."

Corporal Gobrecht fell during a combat mission April 18 when an enemy bullet ripped through his left elbow. He was hospitalized a month during which time he was awarded the Purple Heart.

He returned to active duty May 18 with the 5th Marines, 1st Division.

Corporal Gobrecht went to Vietnam during the latter part of July, 1966, and was in continuous combat operations since then.

June 3 - Hospital Recovery

I came to in the recovery room at First Medical Battalion in Da Nang. Two corpsmen greeted me with big smiles and asked how I was doing? The one corpsman asked if I'd mind him photographing his great stitching techniques when closing up my wounds? I told him I didn't mind whatsoever. He had threaded over a hundred wires and threads throughout my entire left side. Heavy wire had been used wherever the lacerations were wide and deep, while thread was used in areas where future surgery would be required or where the outside appearance would be more noticeable.

My sinuses had been reconstructed and packed with three feet of gauze. Six teeth and part of my gum were missing and Z Plastic Surgery would be needed on the left side of my face. I had 3/4 inch rubber tubing protruding from my back and side to aid in draining away excess fluid build-up. The impact of the concussion and the shrapnel destroyed five thigh muscles of the left leg, three of which ossified into bonelike substance. Fifty or so pieces of residual metal shards would remain within me. Throughout the ordeal of being wounded and the surgery that was required, all total I was given multiple units of blood. All in all, I came through the ordeal better than expected.

The thing that worried me most was how my parents would react to this repeat of bad news. When I was wounded the first time, a Marine came to the house to inform them of my wounding and how I was faring. When my Dad first saw him he thought the worst. The Marine present told him that when someone is killed, the United States Marine Corps sends two messengers instead of one.

WESTERN UNION TELEGRAM

GOV'T PD. WASH, D.C. 6/9/67 448P EDST

MR. & MRS. WILLIAM H. GOBRECHT
R.D.1, HANOVER, PENNSYLVANIA

THIS IS TO CONFIRM THAT YOUR SON LANCE CORPORAL JOHN W. GOBRECHT U.S.M.C. WAS INJURED ON 3 JUNE 67 IN THE VICINITY OF QUANG TIN, REPUBLIC OF VIETNAM. HE SUSTAINED FRAGMENTATION WOUNDS OF THE FACE, LEFT LEG, LEFT ARM, AND BACK. MORTAR ROUND WHILE ON AN OPERATION. HE IS BEING TREATED AT THE STATION HOSPITAL DA NANG. HIS CONDITION AND PROGNOSIS WERE GOOD. YOUR ANXIETY IS REALIZED AND YOU ARE ASSURED THAT HE IS RECEIVING THE BEST OF CARE. HIS MAILING ADDRESS REMAINS THE SAME.

SIGN:
WALLACE M. GREENE
GEN. USMC COMMANDANT OF THE MARINE CORP.

It was the day of my sister's graduation and everyone was getting ready for the big event. My Dad happened to be outside when the government vehicle pulled into the driveway. He immediately saw that the car held two Marines and instantly took it upon himself to prepare my Mother for the impending news. My mother was nine months pregnant, which added an additional concern to the situation. Well, the news turned out to be a lot better than anticipated. Two Marines arrived instead of one because it was my second Purple Heart. The thing that I couldn't understand was that I had been wounded on June 2 and they weren't notified until June 9. I was to find out later that I had been listed as Missing In Action for four days. In reality I was only missing for one day but it took three more days for the Marine Corps to know exactly where I was. Thus, four days.

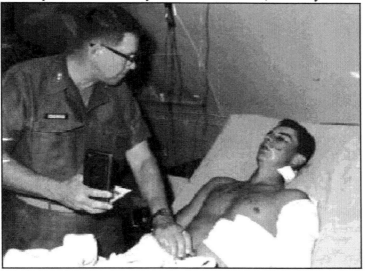

General Cushman presenting Lance Corporal John Gobrecht with his second Purple Heart while participating in Operation Union II.

After new dressings were applied, I was wheeled to the main ward and clean sheets. I rested a good portion of the morning. Sometime near mid-morning I was told that someone was here to see me. The someone turned out to be my gunner, Private First Class Robert Mills. He told me that after leaving him during the assault he had taken a round through both legs and couldn't make it back to friendly lines. He managed to crawl over into some rocks where he hid till morning. Marines sweeping the area found him and immediately medevaced him to First Med in Da Nang.

The doctor said to him, "See, your team leader is quite a bit worse off than you are." Yeah, I thought to myself, "But, I didn't have to spend the entire night in a rice paddy waiting to be rescued." We talked a short while longer before he was wheeled into another ward.

I wouldn't be allowed to leave for the states until I received my forty antibiotic shots and all my injuries scabbed over to stave off infection.

June 18 marked my last day in war torn Vietnam. I departed on an Air Force jet, specially outfitted with stacked hospital beds, to transport the wounded. We stopped in Japan for a fuel stop before continuing on to Andrews Air Force Base near Washington, D.C. Once there, we spent the night and then next morning were placed aboard buses and transported to hospitals nearest our family and home. I arrived at Philadelphia Naval Hospital June 21 where I would remain for the next several months. While there, I would learn to walk again and have the scabs on my thigh torn from my leg three times to eventually bring the level of my scars to a more even level with the surrounding skin. I also required sedation from nightmares I was experiencing.

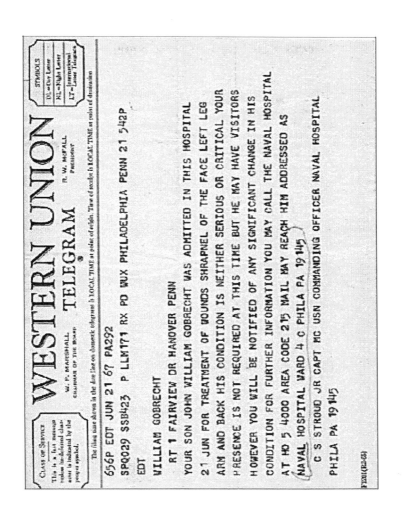

After spending months at the hospital and later working at the Philadelphia Naval Station on light duty, I received orders for Camp Lejeune, North Carolina. I would be transferring to Company A, 2nd Recon Battalion, 2nd Marine Division. While in recon I had the misfortune of doing poorly in a Physical Readiness Test (PRT). I was able to finish but came in last. The Captain gave me holy hell, wanted to know what my problem was and ordered me to report to his office. I reported in and he again wanted to know what the hell was wrong with my attitude. I stated the fact that I had been severely wounded in the war and my thigh wasn't 100%. He told me to drop my drawers. When he saw my damaged thigh, he immediately began apologizing and even commended me on my efforts put forth during the testing. thanked him for his understanding, saluted and departed.

February 16, 1968 saw my departure from the United States Marine Corps, which I was proud to have been a part of. I thank God every day for giving me the opportunity to have served my country with the likes of India Company, 3rd Battalion, Ninth Marines, 3rd Marine Division and especially 2nd Platoon, of Fox Company, 2nd Battalion, 5th Marines, 1st Marine Division. It has been reported that the total KIA and WIA suffered by Foxtrot 2/5 on June 2, 1967 was proportionately more men lost in a single day of combat than any other American infantry company during the entire Vietnam War.

Middle of June 1967 - My father (William Gobrecht) and one of my younger brothers (Jerry) came to see me at the Philadelphia Naval Hospital, while my mother (Gladys Gobrecht) was in the Hanover Hospital giving birth to my youngest sister, Angie.
When I arrived at Philadelphia, I weighed 130 pounds and couldn't walk.

Now it was my brother Terry's turn to go to war. He'll be part of the Marine Air Wing, loading ordinance on attack fighter aircraft located at Chu Lai in I Corps, Vietnam. He would arrive just after the Tet Offensive, approximately the middle of February. If it weren't for close air support, many more infantry Marines would have lost their lives, myself included. Terry would now be the reason why my siblings, Pennie, Jerry, Bonnie, Jay, Lenny, Kathy and Angie will be forced to watch the evening news and the Vietnam War. Not to mention names, one brother in particular told me many years later that he absolutely hated that part of the evening.

I would be the one to drop him off at National Airport to catch a flight that would eventually take him to Vietnam.

TERRY WAYNE GOBRECHT

Terry served in the Marine Corps during the Vietnam War at the Chu Lai Air Base. Gobrecht loaded ordinance on attack fighters and armed the jets. He lost part of a finger while loading ordinance.

Casualties Of Operation Union II

Marines killed in Action - 110
Fox Company 2/5 Killed in Action June 2

Sergeant Gerald Ackley

Lance Corporal Stephen Balters

Lance Corporal Richard Blasen

Private First Class Larry Boatman

Private First Class Jimmy R. Crook

Corporal Victor Driscoll

Lance Corporal Kenneth Endsley

Corporal John Francis

Private First Class Michael McCandless

Private First Class Dennis Monfils

Lance Corporal John R. Painter Jr.

Lance Corporal Benjamin Pelzer II

Corporal Karl B. Rische Jr.

Private First Class James A. Weed

Lance Corporal Jereld Westphal

Corpsman USN Martin

Killed In Action on June 2, but found on June 3

Captain James A. Graham

2nd Lieutenant Straughan D. Kelsey Jr.

Lance Corporal Arthur M. Byrd

Lance Corporal William S. Daugherty

Lance Corporal James J. Deasel Jr.

Corporal Marion Lee Dirickson
 (Captain Graham's radio man)

Corpsman Petty Officer Thomas Donovan

Private First Class Lawson Douglas Gerard

Lance Corporal Robert Reyes Hernandez

Lance Corporal Gary Wayne Kline

Private First Class Keith M. Moser II

Corporal Gary M. O'Brien

Private First Class Robert Richardson

Private First Class Steven E. Scharlach

2nd Lieutenant Charles Joseph Schultz

Private First Class Clifford Shepherd

THE WALL

May this silence through death
Emanating from this great stone slab
Give Strength and hope
To all who tread beside it.

Poem written by John W. Gobrecht in 1991
Former F 2/5 2nd Platoon
1st Marine Division

Marines Wounded In Action 241

Fox Company 2/5 Wounded on June 1, but not evacuated
Private First Class Edwin A. Hawkins

Fox Company 2/5 Wounded on June 2 and medevaced

Private First Class Frank J. Anderson

Lance Corporal Douglas J. Bradstreet

Private First Class Carl E. McNally

Corporal Jimmy L. McClintock

Private First Class David L. McDonald

Lance Corporal John L. Moran

Private First Class Edward T. Miller

Private First Class Gregory N. Vanbuskirk

Lance Corporal John J. Perult

Private First Class Larry D. Wainscott

Lance Corporal Daniel J. Yeutter

Corporal Louis R. Barnes

Private First Class Kenneth H. Cockrell

Corporal Charles Ekker

Lance Corporal Harry Engram

Corporal James R. Hester

Corporal Preston R. Hudson

Staff Sergeant Robert M. Jenkins

Private First Class Floyd J. Johnson

Private Charles B. Kinser Jr.

Corporal Melvin M. Long

Private First Class Lonnie D. Manske

Private Jerold S. Robinson

Private First Class Carl E. Slover
Lance Corporal Carl R. Stone
Lance Corporal Dennis L. Torsch
Lance Corporal John T. Gailey
Private First Class Byron Young Jr.
Private First Class Dennis P. Sheely
Private First Class David (Andy) Anderson
First Lieutenant James B. Scuras
Corporal Cliff Nolan
Corporal Knowles
Corporal Profi
Corporal Ted Verena

Wounded in Action June 2nd, but rescued June 3$_{rd}$
Lance Corporal John W. Gobrecht
Private First Class Robert Mills

Wounded in Action June 2nd, but not evacuated
Private First Class Gary M. Irby
Private First Class Brenton E. MacKinnon
Private First Class Alfred Navarro
Lance Corporal G. L. Pagan
Private First Class MacDalene M. Rojas Jr.
Gunnery Sergeant John S. Green
Corporal Tony Ahinzow
Corporal Tommy L. Dickerson
Private First Class Thomas P. Labarbera

Lance Corporal Timothy L. Wall

Second Lieutenant William A. Knight

Lance Corporal Stephen L. Huber

First Sergeant Cleo E. Lee

Wounded June 3rd

Lance Corporal Joseph L. Hicks

Staff Sergeant Anthony H. Marengo

Corporal Charles W. Conley

Second Platoon suffered a near 100 % casualty rate.

North Vietnamese Army's 2nd Division's Casualty Count sustained during Operation Union II

Killed in Action - 701

Enemy captured – 23

Citations

Captain James A. Graham - The Medal of Honor

Gunnery Sergeant John S. Green - The Navy Cross

Colonel Kenneth Houghton - The Navy Cross

Sergeant Melvin Long - The Navy Cross

Corporal Lloyd Woods - The Navy Cross

Corporal Louis Rick Barnes - The Silver Star

Petty Officer Thomas Donovan - The Silver star

Colonel Kenneth Houghton - The Silver Star

Private First Class Keith Moser II - The Silver Star

Corporal Louis Rick Barnes - Recommended for the Bronze Star With Valor

Lance Corporal John W. Gobrecht - Recommended for the Bronze Star With Valor

All sustaining wounds, would receive the Purple Heart:

For action in both Union I and Union II the Fifth Marines and units under its operational control received The Presidential Unit Citation.

The Presidential Unit Citation (Navy) is awarded to units of the Armed Forces of the United States and cobelligerent nations for extraordinary heroism in action against an armed enemy.

The character of the action must be comparable to that which would merit award of a NAVY CROSS to an individual.

I never think of a Marine but what I think of a man who wants to do more, not less; a man you have to hold back and not shove. As I present you with this citation, I salute you in the name of the freedom that you defend and the honor that you have won for country."

Lyndon B. Johnson, 17 October 1968

President Johnson said the above words as he awarded the Presidential Unit Citation to the entire 5th Marine Regiment for their heroic actions on Operations UNION I, and II in May 1967. (Source information: "United States Marines" published by the United States Marine Corps Division of Information, Feb. 1969).

The President of the United States takes pleasure in presenting the
PRESIDENTIAL UNIT CITATION to the

FIFTH MARINE REGIMENT (REINFORCED)
FIRST MARINE DIVISION (REINFORCED)

for service as set forth in the following

CITATION:

For extraordinary heroism in action against North Vietnamese forces during Operations UNION AND UNION II in the Que Son area, Republic of Vietnam, from 25 April to 5 June 1967. Throughout this period, the 5th Marines (Reinforced) was assigned the mission of destroying the enemy forces, their supplies and equipment. With the initiation of a heavy engagement by a Marine rifle company in the vicinity of La Nga (2), the 5th Marines deployed to exploit the contact.

Despite extremely short notice, the reinforced Regiment moved with alacrity to meet the enemy's challenge. This rapid reaction resulted in the establishment of contact with a well-organized North Vietnamese Army force; once engaged, the 5th Marines tenaciously pursued the enemy over an extensive pattern of rice paddies, hedgerows and fortified hamlets. Unable to disengage while being subjected to relentless pressure, the 21st North Vietnamese Regiment finally made its stand at the hamlet of Phouc Duc (4).

For four days commencing 12 May, the 5th Marines resolutely attacked the fortified enemy positions. Valiantly withstanding heavy enemy mortar barrages and repelling fierce enemy counterattacks, the Marines shattered the entrenched enemy. Operation UNION II was launched on 26 May with a helicopter-borne assault to destroy he withdrawing remnants of the 21st North Vietnamese Regiment.

Attacking aggressively, the 5th Marines uncovered the 3rd North Vietnamese Regiment dug in near Vinh Huy and were met by a withering barrage of mortar, machine-gun and recoilless rifle fire. Resolute in their determination, the Marines continued to maintain pressure and, at nightfall, launched a bold right attack which ruptured the enemy's defenses and drove the tattered vestiges of the North Vietnamese unit from the field.

UNION and UNION II inflicted over three thousand enemy casualties and eliminated the 2nd North Vietnamese Army Division as a combat force to be reckoned with for many months. By their aggressive fighting spirit, superb tactical skill, steadfastness under fire, consummate professionalism and countless acts of individual heroism, the officers and men of the 5th Marine Regiment (Reinforced) upheld the highest traditions of the Marine Corps, and the United States Naval service.

Medal of Honor Recipients

I had the privilege of serving with three Medal of Honor recipients and would like to recognize them in this composition. One was when I served with India Company 3/9, 3rd Marine Division and two when I served with Fox Company 2/5, 1st Marine Division. Their citations follow:

The President of the United States takes pride in presenting the Medal of Honor posthumously to

SECOND LIEUTENANT JOHN P. BOBO
UNITED STATES MARINE CORPS

For service as set forth in the following

CITATION

For the gallantry and intrepidity at the risk of his life above the call of duty as Weapons Platoon Commander, Company I, Third Battalion, Ninth Marines, Third Marine Division, in Quang Tri Providence, Republic of Vietnam, on 30 March 1967. Company I was establishing night ambush sites when the command group was attacked by a reinforced North Vietnamese company supported by heavy automatic weapons and mortar fire. Lieutenant Bobo immediately organized a hasty defense and moved from position to position encouraging the out numbered Marine despite the murderous enemy fire. Recovering a rocket launcher from among the friendly casualties, he organized a new launcher team and directed its fire into the enemy gun positions. When an exploding enemy mortar round severed Lieutenant Bobo's right leg below the knee, he refused to be evacuated and insisted upon being placed in a firing position to cover the movement of the command group to a better location. With a web belt around his leg, jammed into the dirt to curtail the bleeding, he remained in this position and delivered devastating fire into the ranks of the enemy attempting to overrun the Marines. Lieutenant Bobo was mortally wounded while firing his weapon into the main point of the enemy attack but his valiant spirit inspired his men to heroic efforts, and his tenacious stand enabled the command group to gain a protective position where it repulsed the enemy onslaught. Lieutenant Bobo's superb leadership, dauntless courage, and bold initiative reflected great credit upon himself and upheld the highest traditions of the Marine Corps and the United States Naval Service. He gallantly gave his life for his country.

(Signed) Lyndon B. Johnson

The President of the United States takes pride in presenting the MEDAL OF HONOR posthumously to

CAPTAIN JAMES A. GRAHAM
UNITED STATES MARINE CORPS

For service as set forth in the following

CITATION:

For conspicuous gallantry and intrepidity at the risk of his own life above and beyond the call of duty. During Operation Union II, the $1_{st\ Battalion,}$ 5th Marines, consisting of Companies A and D, with Captain Graham's company attached, launched an attack against an enemy occupied position with two companies assaulting and one in reserve. Company F, a leading company, was proceeding across a clear paddy area 1,000 meters wide, attacking toward the assigned objective, when it came under fire from mortars and small arms which immediately inflicted a large number of casualties. Hardest hit by the enemy fire was the 2nd platoon of Company F, which was pinned down in the open paddy area by intense fire from 2 concealed machine guns. Forming an assault unit from members of his small company headquarters, Captain Graham boldly led a fierce assault through the second platoon's position, forcing the enemy to abandon the first machine gun position, thereby relieving some of the pressure on his second platoon, and enabling evacuation of the wounded to a more secure area.

Resolute to silence the second machine gun, which continued its devastating fire, Captain Graham's small force stood steadfast in its hard won enclave. Subsequently, during the afternoon's fierce fighting, he suffered 2 minor wounds while personally accounting for an estimated 15 enemy killed. With the enemy position remaining invincible upon each attempt to withdraw to friendly lines, and although knowing that he had no chance of survival, he chose to remain with 1 man who could not be moved due to the seriousness of his wounds. The last radio transmission from Captain Graham reported that he was being assaulted by a force of 25 enemy soldiers; he died while protecting himself and the wounded man he chose not to abandon. Captain Graham's actions throughout the day were a series of heroic achievements. His outstanding courage, superb leadership and indomitable fighting spirit undoubtedly saved the second platoon from annihilation and reflected great credit upon himself, the Marine Corps, and the U.S. Naval service. He gallantly gave his life for his country.

(Signed) LYNDON B. JOHNSON

Return To Union II

June 2, 2000 - 33 years to the day of Foxtrot's Union II battle saw Major John Graham, USMC and his sister Jennifer visiting the area where their father, Captain James Graham gave the ultimate sacrifice so others might live. Somewhere on Hill B, near Huy Vinh 2, a small token was buried, followed by a brief ceremony. The view overlooks the rice paddy where so many hearts were broken, but where respect for the fighting men will live on forever.

The President of the United States in the name of Congress takes pride in presenting the MEDAL OF HONOR posthumously to

PRIVATE FIRST CLASS MELVIN E. NEWLIN
UNITED STATES MARINE CORPS

For services as set forth in the following

CITATION:

For conspicuous gallantry and intrepidity at the risk of his life above and beyond the call of duty while serving as a machine gunner attached to the first platoon, Company F, Second Battalion, Fifth Marines, First Marine Division, in the Republic of Vietnam on 3 and 4 July 1967. Private Newlin with four other Marines, was manning a key position on the perimeter of the Nong Son outpost when the enemy launched a savage and well coordinated mortar and infantry assault, seriously wounding him and killing his four comrades. Propping himself against his machine gun, he poured a deadly accurate stream of fire into the charging ranks of the Viet Cong. Though repeatedly hit by small arms fire, he twice repelled enemy attempts to overrun his position. During the third attempt, a grenade explosion wounded him again and knocked him to the ground unconscious. The Viet Cong guerrillas, believing him dead, bypassed him and continued their assault on the main force. Meanwhile, Private Newlin regained consciousness, crawled back to his weapon, and brought it to bear on the rear of the enemy causing havoc and confusion among them. Spotting the enemy attempting to bring a captured 106 recoiless weapon to bear on other Marine positions, he shifted his fire, inflicting heavy casualties on the enemy and preventing them from firing the captured weapon. He then shifted his fire back to the primary enemy force, causing the enemy to stop their assault on the Marine bunkers and to once again attack his machine gun position. Valiantly fighting off two more enemy assaults, he firmly held his ground until mortally wounded. Private Newlin had single-handedly broken up and disorganized the entire enemy assault force, causing them to lose momentum and delaying them long enough for his fellow Marines to organize a defense and beat off their secondary attack. His indomitable courage, fortitude, and unwavering devotion to duty in the face of almost certain death reflected great credit upon himself and the Marine Corps and upheld the highest traditions of the United States Naval Service.

/S/ RICHARD M. NIXON

The Fallen Soldier Table

When I attended a Unit Reunion Dinner for Foxtrot 2/5 in Washington D.C. 2008. I came away with emotions that can't be described. Near the head table, but slightly off to the side and easily seen was a small round table set specifically for the fallen soldier. Each individual part of the setting symbolizes something significant and is described in a very somber ritual to those attending. The ceremony ends with a toast and or prayer to The Fallen Soldier.

1. Place a small table near the head table, but slightly off to the side and out of the way, but where guests can all see it.
2. Spread a white table cloth making sure that it is straight and even. Represents purity of intentions to respond to their country's call to arms.
3. Set one place, with a clean place mat, plate, bread plate, cloth napkin and utensils. This setting represents your wish that the fallen men and women of the armed forces could be present at this happy occasion with you.
4. Insert a simple white candle into a simple candle holder and place it to one side of the center of the table, beyond the place setting. The candle represents the light of hope.
5. Place a long-stemmed rose into a simple bud vase and place it to the other side of the table from the candle. The rose represents the families who love and keep faith with the men and women who serve.
6. Tie a ribbon into a bow on the vase and place it on the other side of the table from the candle. A red ribbon symbolizes the memory of and the search for those missing in action.

7. Invert the wine glass and place it upside down to the right of the plate. This represents that the fallen soldier will not be able to participate in the happy toasts at the event.
8. Place a lemon wedge on the bread plate. It represents the bitter loss of the life of the fallen soldier.
9. Sprinkle the salt over the lemon and the bread plate. The salt represents tears.
10. Place an empty chair at the table in front of the place setting. This represents the missing comrade.

I salute and give a toast to all my fallen brothers of Foxtrot 2/5. There isn't a day goes by that I don't think about June 2, 1967 and tears are sometimes shed. I truly miss you.

God Bless and SEMPER FI.

Letters

June 3, 1967   9:00 P.M.

Dear John,

    I hope this letter finds you doing alright, and I wish I could be there with you, but I guess I'll have to wait: right??

    Well I just got through inventorying your seabag: and I put your record player in it and also your letters and etc.

    I didn't send your records, because there wasn't much room for anything else; and if you want me to send them to you I will soon as possible!!

    Well it looks like we're getting back to normal: and we're supposed to go on another operation the 15th of June; I think they're trying to get me killed!!

    I'll tell you now I'll not go out in the field again; if I have to shoot myself; I can't take it any longer and you should know why!!

    John I guess I'll close for now and try to write my wife, and if it's possible for you to write; please do, alright??

    Take care of yourself and let me know how you're doing and if I make it out of this alive, I'll go see you! !

    Good night and good-bye for now and take care of yourself; and pray.

P.S. Write Soon

    A friend and Buddy Always, Perry

June 5, 1967   3:30 P.M.

Dear John,

Well here I am alive and in pretty good health: but I wish I could be with you!

After the battle I tried to find you, but they told me that the whole second squad of guns had been wiped out and I'll tell you now I felt like crying!!

I guess you're home now or at least in good care by a nice looking nurse and I sure hope you feel good or at least better!!

I lost two men, but they'll be alright and I guess that's all I could ask for; right??

O'Brien was killed and Barnes was wounded pretty bad and the rest were wounded, but we had 34 KIAs and I was sick!!

If I ever have to pick up another dead person I'll go crazy as a bat and that's no lie! !

We finally got back to good old An Hoa and it seemed as if everyone was gone and I felt like a lone wolf!!

Boy I was sure glad to know you made it and I'm glad to know you're going back to the states; I only wish I could be there with you !!

I'm supposed to be Section Leader now, but all we got left are eight men and three machine guns??!!

Well enough for this place; I've got your records and record player and if I get enough money, I'll send it to you as soon as possible; alright??

Well I guess I'll say good-bye old buddy; take care of yourself and write me from (life) alright?? May God Bless and keep you safe and I hope to see you soon!!

P.S. Write Soon

    A friend Always, Perry

June 20, 1967   1:30 P.M.

Hi John,

Well here I am still in Vietnam and it looks as if I'll be here quite awhile yet, but each day brings me a little closer to getting home; right??

I just got off R & R……..

………Hawaii looked the same way I left it twice before, but it was nice to do as I liked for awhile!!

It won't be too much longer before I'll be home; but still I get the feeling they're trying to get me killed; isn't that funny????!!

Well I guess you're out of the hospital by now; but you still got a few cuts on you; right??

Corporal Hull has your diary and I'll get it and send it to you as soon as possible, if not sooner ok??

I just phoned the company office a few minutes ago and I can stay here at Da Nang one more day and I wish I could stay longer, but it would be asking too much, right??

The company is going to the coal mine (Nong Song) tomorrow and I guess they'll stay there a month or so and I hope there are no V.C. out there; but it's impossible, right??

Boy I'll sure be glad to get out of this place and I was glad to hear you made it out, but it's the hard way, right??

I want to know where you're at and also send me your address and write whenever possible; alright??

Well I guess I'll close for now, but I'll write whenever possible and I'll let you know how the outfit's doing!!

May God bless and keep you safe till we meet once more!!

P.S. Write

A friend always, Perry

July 2, 1967   6:30 P.M.

Dear John,

Well, I finally received a letter from you and it sure made me feel good to know you're alright.

I hate to tell you this, but 2nd Platoon isn't there anymore, only six men made it out after the fire fight!!

I guess I was pretty lucky and I hope God will lead and guide me through all this and the rest of us!!

I guess you're pretty messed up; but after the wounds heal, you'll be as good as new, nobody, will ever know you were hit!!

I feel the same way you do about this place, I'm glad you're in the world again, for good!!

Oh, I received a letter from your people and they told me they didn't know where you were, but I guess by now they know, right??

John I'll give you Barnes' address and I'll try and get Roth's for you; and also a few others alright??

If you can write Calvin he can give you Roth's address and some of the old guys; alright??

I hope those will help a little and if you ever need anyone's address I'll see if I can help you; alright??

Tell your people I said "Hello" and to keep what I write to themselves; and I'll see you soon; I hope!!

Well I guess I'll close this letter for now and I'll try to write every chance so keep in touch; ok??

Oh' ' Your diary is on its way to your home; and no one had a chance to read it so don't worry, alright??

Take care of yourself; and if you are near Georgia, you had better stop; and we'll go hunting awhile; if it's alright with you ! !

Well take care Vietnam Casualty and don't step on any pins. May God bless and keep you safe and write every chance!!

P.S. Write

        A friend and Buddy always,
        Perry Jones

Bibliography

BOOKS:

Brown, Lieutenant Colonel David B. (Ret.) and Holmes, Tiffany Brown, *Battlelines*, Lincoln Nebraska: Universe, Inc. 2005.

Culbertson, John J., *A Sniper In The Arizona;* 2nd Battalion, 5th Marines, in the Arizona territory, 1967. New York: Ivy Books, 1999, The Ballantine Publishing Company.

Currey, Cecil B., *Victory At Any Cost*, The Genius of Vietnam's General Vo Nguyen Giap, Washington; Brassey's, Inc., 1997.

Gobrecht, Wilbur J., Editor and Chairman, members: Edward J. Gobrecht, SR., Anna Gobrecht Sheffer, Lester L, Gobrecht, David C. Houck, Jeune Gobrecht Seibert, Donald Sterner and Glenn E. Gobrecht, *Gobrecht Family History:* History of the John Christopher Gobrecht Family in America 1753-1977. No Publisher.

Lanning, Michael Lee and Ray Williams Stubbs, *Inside Force Recon*; Recon Marines In Vietnam. New York: Ivy Books, 1989, pages 112-113.

Lehrack, Otto J., *Road of 10,000 Pains,* The Destruction of the 2nd NVA Division by the U.S. Marines, page 1, 1967, Zenith Press, 2010.

Scruggs, Jan C. and Joel L. Swerdlow. *To Heal A Nation:* The Vietnam Veterans Memorial. New York: Harper and Row Publishers, 1985.

Shulimson, Jack, *U.S. Marines In Vietnam: An Expanding War, 1966*. History and Museums Division Headquarters, U.S. Marine Corps, Washington D.C. 1982. LCC No. 82-600567.

Telfer, Major Gary L., USMC, Lieutenant Colonel Lane Rogers, USMC and V. Keith Fleming, Jr., *U.S. Marines In Vietnam; Fighting The North Vietnamese.* History and Museums Division Headquarters, U.S. Marine Corps, Washington D.C. 1984. LCC No. 77-604776.

Summers, Jr., Colonel Harry G. *Vietnam War Almanac,* New York: Facts On File Publications, 1985.

Weiss, Stephen, Clark Dougan, David Fulghum, Donald Kennedy and the editors of Boston Publishing Company. *The Vietnam Experience: A War Remembered,* pages 52-53, Boston, MA, Boston Publishing Company.

PERIODICALS:

Anon. *Area Marine Is Wounded Second Time,* Hanover Evening Sun Vol. 109, No. 75, June 9, 1967 Pages 1 and 6.

Arnold, 2nd Lieutenant R.E. *During 3-Hour Battle Kit Carson Scout Kills 31 Former Comrades,* Sea Tiger Vol. III, No. 24 (June 16, 1967), pages 1 and 12.

Citations: Military Sealift Command (U.S.Navy)

Contested Rice Paddy, June 2. Pages 25,27,31,37, and 41. *Ambush At Union II,* Marine Corps Gazette, Nov. 1989.

Department of Defense. NAVPERS 15214, NAVMC 2608, Know Your Enemy: The Viet Cong. 1966.

Fleet Marine Force Pacific, Department Of The Navy, MCBul 3480. A Marine's Guide To The Republic of Vietnam. June 1, 1967.

Fox 2/5 Association Newsletter, Fall 2008, pages 7 and 8.

Official Military Manuals and Publications.

Personal Papers and Source Notes:

1st Battalion, 5th Marines, 1st Marine Division (Rein.) FM5, After Action Report, Operation Union II (Search and Destroy) 1/5 Frag Order 28, 29, 30, 31, 32, 34, 35, 36, 37, 38 - 67 Division 3480.1 3-CHB/g1k 3480 16 June, 1967.

2nd Battalion, 5th Marines, 1st Marine Division, Company F, Unit Diary RUC 11175, May and June 1967.

2nd Battalion, 5th Marines, 1st Marine Division (Rein), FHF.

After Action Report, Operation Union II (Search and Destroy) 2/5 Frag Order 17-67 and 18-67 3/MCO/wfm 8 June 1967.

3rd Battalion, 5th Marines, 1st Marine Division, FMF, After Action Report, 3 Operation Union II (Search and Destroy) 3/5 Frag Order 28-67 and 32-67 and Division Order 3480.1 3 CBW Pib 3121 II June, 1967.

Internet:

GlobalSecurity.org

Personal Diary:

Gobrecht, John W., July 1966 through June 1967 Vietnam.

Letters:

Perry Jerry Jones - June 3, 5, 30, and July, 1967.

Telephone Conversations:

Perry Jones - 1991

Rick Barnes - 1991

Poem:

Skypeck, George L. "Soldier"

Photography Credits:

Page 39, Sgt. Gary Thomas, Sea Tiger, Jets Hit Enemy Positions, 1967.

Page 45, USMC, 1967.

Page 110, Kristyn Hartman, 2008.

Back Cover Graphic: "Know Your Enemy: The Viet Cong (DoD Gen-20) - This official Department of Defense publication is for the use of personnel in the military services.

Glossary Of Terms And Abbreviations

AK-47 - Russian or Chinese made automatic assault rifle.

An Hoa - A battalion area of the 5th Marines approximately 18 miles southwest of Da Nang.

ARVN - Army of the Republic of Vietnam (South Vietnam).

B-52 - Boeing Stratofortress (heavy bomber).

BAR - Browning Automatic Rifle.

Booby-Trap - Hidden device to cause injury.

Bunker - Protected and reinforced gun positions.

C-4 - A Pliable plastic explosive.

C-Rats - Canned food or rations.

CH-46-A - Sea knight, a tandem-rotor transport helicopter.

Capt. - Captain, usually a company commander.

Chieftain - Elder male of a particular village.

Chopper - Slang for helicopter.

CO - Commanding Officer.

Cobra Gun ships - AH-1 G Attack helicopters.

Col. - Colonel, usually a regimental commander.

Cold LZ - Landing zone with enemy personnel absent

Cpl. - Corporal.

Dike - Embankments in rice fields to control the level of water irrigation.

Doc - Navy corpsman or Army medic.

DMZ - Demilitarized Zone separating North and South Vietnam.

Fixed Wing - All stationary winged aircraft.

Flares (illumination) - phosphorus pyrotechnics suspended under parachutes, released from aircraft, artillery and mortars.

Guerrillas - Local villagers and Viet Cong using harassing hit and run tactics.

Gun Ships - C-47 Gooneybird, AC-47, AC-119, C-130 Hercules, AC-130 all of which were nicknamed Dragonships, Puffs and Spookies.

Gun Team - A crew of three or four men operating a machine gun.

Gunny - Gunnery Sergeant.

Hardcore - North Vietnamese troops.

Ho - North Vietnam's Ho Chi Minh.

Ho Chi Minh Trail - Large network paths used by the North Vietnamese Army to move from North Vietnam through Laos and Cambodia into South Vietnam.

Hot LZ - Enemy occupying the landing zone.

House Bunker - Underground chamber bomb shelter.

I Corp. - Northern most area of South Vietnam bordering the DMZ.

II Corp. - Area of South Vietnam just south of I Corp.

III MAF - 3rd Marine Amphibious Force.

Incoming - Hostile fire.

John Wayne - Famous Hollywood Actor portrayed in action and war movies.

John Wayne Assault - Marine walking at a fast pace, slightly crouched, with weapon held in firing position, showing no fear when assaulting enemy positions, as portrayed in movies.

KIA - Killed in action.

Kit Carson Scout - Former Viet Cong defecting to South Vietnam.

LCpl. - Lance Corporal.

Leathernecks - United States Marines.

Lt. - Lieutenant, usually a platoon commander.

LZ - Landing Zone.

Man Down - Wounded.

Man Down Hard - Dead.

Mayday, Mayday - International, radio telephone distress signal used by ships and aircraft.

Medevac - Medical evacuation.

Napalm - Jellied gasoline.

Noncoms - Noncommissioned officers.

NVA - North Vietnamese Army.

Outgoing - Friendly fire mission.

P-38 - Government issue can opener.

PFC - Private First Class.

Phantom - Primary attack, supersonic fighter jet such as the F-4.

PPB - Platoon Patrol Base.

Puff - AC-47, AC-119 and AC-130 known also as dragon-ships and Spookies.

Punj i Stakes - pointed pieces of bamboo or steel smeared with human feces.

Purple Heart - Awarded exclusively for wounds suffered in combat.

Pvt. - Private.

Recon - Reconnaissance.

Rice Paddy - Rice field.

RPG - Rocket Propelled Grenade.

RVN - Republic of Vietnam.

Sea Knights - CH-46 transport, tandem rotor helicopters.

Sgt. - Sergeant.

Shrapnel - Shards of metal from an explosive device.

Spider Trap - Sunken pits harboring snipers.

Spooky - AC-47, AC11FO and AC-130 gun ships also know as Dragon-ship and Puff.

Sucking Chest Wound - Whole in chest preventing lungs from holding air, causing them to collapse.

VC - Viet Cong.

Villa - French name for village.

Ville - Refers to village in Vietnam.

WIA - Wounded In Action.

✶ ✶ ✶ ✶ ✶ ✶ ✶ ✶ ✶ ✶ ✶ ✶ ✶ ✶ ✶ ✶ ✶

JOHN W. GOBRECHT served with India Company, 3rd Battalion, 9th Marine Regiment, 3rd Marine Division at An Hoa, Republic of Vietnam, from July 31 to November 27, 1966 and Fox Company 2nd Battalion, 5th Marine Regiment, 1st Marine Division, at An Hoa, Republic of Vietnam, from November 28, 1966 to June 20, 1967. Lance Corporal Gobrecht served as a machine-gun team leader, MOS 0331, on Operation Union II. He was wounded in action, earning two Purple Hearts. He was awarded The Vietnam Service Medal with Device, Vietnam Campaign Medal, Purple Heart with Device, National Defense Medal and Presidential Unit Citation, Navy Unit Commendation. Lance Corporal Gobrecht received an honorable discharge February 16, 1968 from the United States Marine Corps.

* * * * * * * * * * * * * * * *

In 2008, at Foxtrot 2/5's Unit Reunion in Washington, D.C., I had the good fortune of reuniting with guys I hadn't seen for nearly forty years. We talked about the good and the bad times at which time some tears were shed. Hank Januchowski (Ski), my former Squad Leader, brought his beautiful daughter in from Chicago. Norm Osborne (Ozzie), came in from New Jersey. He had been wounded prior to Union II. Rick Barnes brought his entire family along, and I believe at the time he was living in Florida. This was the first time we were able to get together since our fight for survival in the rice paddy in 1967. I thoroughly enjoyed spending time with him and his family. Before leaving the reunion, we were able to have a picture taken of the four of us. We were all former machine gunners of Foxtrot 2/5.

Photo Courtesy of Kristyn Hartman.

Pictured left to right: Hank Januchowski (Ski), Rick Barnes, Norm Osborne (Ozzie), John Gobrecht.

Notes

Colonel Cu's information was further substantiated by a Sting Ray Patrol*, code name Team Classmate, of one such patrol, in support of Operation Union II on May 26, 1967 reported the following oral history tape:

"At 0900 we saw five VC step off the trail on the high ground side. About 50 meters above the trail they set down their packs and weapons and appeared observing the trail from which they had just come. We called in artillery, had good coverage of the area and we noted one VC limping away. Again we called artillery and brought it right on top of the man ... 25 minutes later we observed two VC by a large dike full of water. We called another artillery mission on them and got one confirmed KIA - we could see his body on the dike and one probable. Only 40 minutes later we observed five VC moving up the hill toward our position carrying packs and weapons. We call a fire mission right on the target."

* Sting Ray was a term used by small unit 1st Force Recon Patrols. Get into the bush, locate the enemy and destroy him with artillery and air power specifically assigned to that particular mission.

On the same encounter, Team Classmate reported seeing one enemy soldier who was approximately six feet tall and weighing about 250 pounds. They said he neither looked nor walked like the VC he accompanied, and thought that maybe he was a mainland Chinese advisor.*

Accumulation of all data, initiated III MAF into organizing and activating another multi-battalion operation. The operation would be code named - Union II.

Photograph: It is my opinion that the photograph on page 45 was taken on May 30, while the Marines of Fox Company 2/5 were entering into their portion of the Union II operation and not in June, as documented below the photograph.

I also think that the Marine shown foremost in the photograph is/was Corporal Perry Jerry Jones of Ellabell, Georgia. He was the machine-gun squad leader for 3_{rd} Platoon of Fox 2/5.

* There are far more reports than confirmations of Chinese advisors from other communist bloc countries being spotted with the enemy. Although there is little doubt that some of these sightings were reliable, it should be understood that ethnic Chinese and other nationalities were native to North Vietnam and were equally subject to the draft.

United States Marine Corps Chain of Command

Unit	Marines	Typical Commander
1. fireteam	3+1 (4)	corporal
2. squad/section	8 – 13	sergeant
3. platoon	26 – 64	second/first lieutenant
4. company	80 – 225	captain/major
5. battalion	300 – 1,300	lieutenant colonel/colonel
6. regiment/brigade	3,000 – 5,000	lieutenant colonel/colonel brigadier general
7. division	10,000 – 19,000	major general
8. Marine Corps	165,000 – 203,000	lieutenant general (four stars) Commandant (a Joint Chief of Staff) (four star general)

The Marine Corps usually uses the rule of three, such as three fire teams make up a squad or three battalions make up a regiment and so on. There are exceptions to this rule, adding units as needed.

It must be noted that while I served in Vietnam during 1966 and 1967, our unit numbers were usually one-half to two-thirds full strength. All above numbers are merely estimates.

Index

45 caliber pistol - 40
57 Recoiless Rifle - 36
106 Recoiless Rifle (weapon) - 90

A

AC-47 Gunships - 56
Ackley, Sergeant Gerald - 47, 75
Ahinzow, Corporal Tony - 78
AK-47 - 35-36, 44
Anderson (Andy), Private First Class David - 78
Anderson, Private First Class Frank J. - 77
Antenna Valley - 5, 19
Arizona Valley - 5
Army of the Republic of Vietnam (South) - 7, 9, 11, 25-26, 29
    1st ARVN Range Group - 14, 25
    6th ARVN Regiment - 14, 25

B

Balters. Lance Corporal Stephen - 75
Barnes, Corporal Louis Rick - 9, 35, 38, 40, 43-44, 47-49, 51-52, 60-61, 77, 81, 96, 98, 103, 110
Blasen, Lance Corporal Richard - 23, 57, 75
Boatman, Private First Class Larry - 75
Bobo, Second Lieutenant John P. - 86
Booby Traps - 6, 22
Bronze Star - 81
Brown, Lieutenant Colonel David (Retired) - 36

Browning Automatic Rifle (BAR) - 31
Byrd, Lance Corporal Arthur M. - 76

C

C-4 Plastic Explosive - 33
Calvin - 98
Camp Lejeune - 71
CH-34 helicopter - 5
CH-46A Sea Knight helicopter - 21, 27, 29
CH-53 Sikorsky helicopter - 60-61
Chinese advisor - 112
Cockrell, Private First Class Kenneth H. - 77
Cong, Major Dao - 43
Conley, Corporal Charles W. - 79
Crook, Private First Class Jimmy - 75
Cu Ban - 5
Cu, Colonel Haynh - 7

D

Daugherty, Lance Corporal William S. - 76
Deasel, Jr., Lance Corporal James J. - 76
Dirickson, Corporal Marion Lee - 47-48, 76
Donovan, Petty Officer Thomas - 48-49, 61, 76. 81
Dragonships - 56
Driscoll, Corporal Victor - 75

E

Ekker, Corporal Charles - 77
Endsley, Lance Corporal Kenneth - 75
Engram, Lance Corporal Harry - 77
Esslinger, Lieutenant Colonel - 14, 25, 27

F

F-4 Phantom - 61

First Medical Battalion - 65, 67
Fowler, Gordon - 55
Francis, Corporal John - 75

G

Gailey, Lance Corporal John T. - 78
Gerard, Private First Class Lawson Douglas - 76
Giap, General - 2
Gobrecht, Angie F. - 72-73
Gobrecht, Bonnie S. - 73
Gobrecht, Gladys M. - 72
Gobrecht, Jay A. - 73
Gobrecht, Jerry L. - 72-73
Gobrecht, Kathy J. - 73
Gobrecht, Lance Corporal John W. - i-ii, 45, 47, 65, 69, 72, 76, 78, 81
Gobrecht, Lenny R. - 73
Gobrecht, Pennie M. - 73
Gobrecht, Terry W. - 72-73
Gobrecht, William H. - 65, 72
Graham, Captain James A. - 14, 29, 38, 43, 47-48, 51-52, 62, 76, 81, 88-89
Graham, Major John - 89
Green, Gunnery Sergeant John S. - 48, 51, 78, 81

H

Haley, Corporal Pat (Water Bu) - 40
Hartman, Kristyn - 110
Hawkins, Private First Class Edwin A. - 77
Hernandez, Lance Corporal Robert Reyes - 76
Hester, Corporal James R. - 77
Hicks, Lance Corporal Joseph L. - 79
Hiep Duc - 8
Hilgartner, Lieutenant Colonel - 14, 25, 38, 61
Hill 55 - 5, 51
Ho Chi Minh - 1
Ho Chi Minh Trail - 7, 12, 25
Houghton, Colonel Kenneth - 14, 28-29, 81
Huber, Lance Corporal Stephen A. - 79
Hull, Corporal - 97

I

I Corp - 3, 6-7, 55, 72
II Corp - 9

III Marine Amphibious Force (III MAF) - 7, 14, 235, 112
Irby, Private First Class Gary M. - 78

J

Jackson, Lieutenant Colonel Mallet – 14, 52
Januchowski, Hank (Ski) - 110
Jenkins, Staff Sergeant Robert M. - 77
Johnson, Dean - 60
Johnson, President Lyndon B. - 82, 87. 89
Johnson, Private First Class Floyd J. - 77
Jones, Corporal Perry Jerry -9, 40, 52, 95-99, 112

K

Kelsey, Second Lieutenant Straughan - 38, 76
Kinh, Kit Carson Scout - 39
Kinser, Jr., Private Charles B. - 77
Kline, Lance Corporal Gary Wayne - 76
Knight, Second Lieutenant William A. - 79
Knowles, Corporal - 78

L

Labarbera, Private First Class Tom - 48, 78
Landing Zone Eagle - 27
Laurence, Colonel Benedict E. (U.S. Army, Retired) - ii
Lee, First Sergeant Cleo E. - 79
Lehrack, Otto J. - 2
Liberty Bridge - 5
Lien Kit 106 – 25, 28
Long, Corporal Melvin - 40, 77, 81
Ly Ly River - 8
LZ - 27, 29, 45, 55, 59, 61

M

M-16 rifle - 22, 38
M-60 machine gun - 22
MacKinnon, Private First Class Brenton E. - 78
Manske, Private First Class Lonnie D. - 77
Marengo, Staff Sergeant Anthony - 39, 79

Martin, Corpsman USN - 75
McCandless, Private First Class Michael - 75
McClintock, Corporal Jimmy - 77
McDonald, Private First Class David L. - 77
McNally, Private First Class Carl E. - 77
Medal of Honor – 41, 51, 62, 81, 85-86, 88, 90
Medevac – 36, 51, 60-61, 70, 77
Miller, Private First Class Edward T. - 77
Mills, Private First Class Robert - 43, 61, 69, 78
Monfils, Private First Class Dennis - 75
Moran, Lance Corporal John L. - 77
Moser, II, Private First Class Keith M. - 76, 81
My Loc 2 – 5

N

Navarro, Private First Class Alfred - 78
Navy Cross – 81-82
Newlin, Private First Class Melvin Earl - 41, 62, 90-91
Nixon, President Richard M. - 91
Nolan, Corporal Cliff - 78
Nong Son - 19, 41, 62, 90, 97
North Vietnam - 2, 7, 12, 25
North Vietnamese Army (NVA) – 2, 5-9, 12-13, 15,19, 25, 27, 28, 35-36, 38, 41, 43-44, 48-49, 51-53, 58-59, 61-62, 79, 83
   2nd North Vietnamese Army Division – 9, 12, 13, 15, 25, 28, 44, 62, 83
     3rd NVA Regiment - 9, 15
     21st NVA Regiment - 9, 15
     31st NVA Regiment - 15, 43
     3rd Viet Cong Regiment – 15
     1st Viet Cong Regiment - 15 (arrives August 9, 1967)

O

O'Brien, Corporal Gary M. – 47-49, 52, 76, 96
Operations   (Marine)
  Beaver Cage - 11
  Cochise - 11
  Colorado - 11

    Double Eagle - 11
    Harvest Moon - 11
    Kansas - 12
    Swift - 13
    Tuscaloosa - 51
    Union I - 9, 11, 19, 21, 23, 62-63
    Union II - 1-2, 6, 9, 12, 14, 19, 21, 23, 25, 31, 33, 35, 43, 55, 61-62, 69, 75, 79, 81, 83, 88-89, 111-112
        (Army)
    Wallowa - 13
    Wheeler - 13
Osborne, Norm (Ozzie) – 110

P

Pagan, Lance Corporal G. L. - 78
Painter, Jr., Lance Corporal John R. - 75
Pelzer, II, Lance Corporal Benjamin - 75
Perult, Lance Corporal John J. - 77
Philadelphia Naval Hospital - 70-72
Phu Lac 6 - 5, 22
Presidential Unit Citation - 81-83
Profi, Corporal - 78
Puff the Magic Dragon - 56
Purple Heart - 65, 69, 81

Q

Quang Nam Province - 8, 13, 65
Quang Tin Province - 8, 13, 68
Quang Tri Province - 86
Que Son Basin (valley) - 1-2, 6-9, 11-12, 19, 25, 55, 63

R

Richardson, Private First Class Robert - 76
Rische, Jr., Corporal Karl B. - 75
Robinson, Private Jerold S. - 77
Rojas, Jr., Private First Class MacDalene M. - 78
Roth - 98
RPG (rocket propelled grenade) - 36

S

Sanctuary Hospital Ship - 19
Scharlach, Private First Class Steven E. - 76
Schultz, 2nd Lieutenant Charles - 76
Scuras, First Lieutenant James B. - 78
Sheely, Private First Class Dennis P. - 78
Shepherd, Private First Class Clifford – 76
Silver Star - 81
Skypeck, George L. – back cover
Slover, Private First Class Carl E. - 78
Song Vu Gia Valley - 5
Son Thu Bon - 5
South Vietnam - 1-2, 7, 62, 65
  An Hoa Combat Base - 5-7, 19, 21-23, 29, 41, 51, 96
  Chu Lai - 7, 19, 51, 72-73
  Da Nang - 5, 7, 19, 60-61, 65, 67, 70, 97
  Hue City - 63
  Nong Son - 19, 41, 62, 90, 97
  Nui Loc Son - 7-8, 27
  Thang Binh - 8, 25
  Tam Ky - 7-8, 12, 19, 25, 29
  Vinh Huy – 35, 44, 83
Spooky - 56
Sting, Ray - 111
Stone, Lance Corporal Carl R. - 78

T

TAOR - 5
Team Classmate – 14, 111-112
Tet Offensive (1968) - 1, 72
Thoa, Major General Hoang - 25
Thompson Sub Machine Gun - 22
Torsch, Lance Corporal Dennis L. - 78
Trung, Major General Dan Quang - 25
Truong Son Trail – 25

U

U. S. Marine Corps Chain of Command - 113
U. S. Marine Units and Commanders – 14-15
   1st Division - Major General Donn Robertson - 6, 13-14, 21, 65, 72, 76, 85, 90, 109
      1st Force Reconnaissance-Team Classmate – 12, 14, 111
      5th Marine Regiment - Colonel Houghton – 6, 12-15, 21, 25, 27-29, 35, 45, 55, 61-62, 65, 72, 81-83, 88, 90-91
         1st Battalion (Maneuver groups for III MAF) - 12, 21
         1st Battalion - Lieutenant Colonel Hilgartner - 14, 21, 25, 35, 38, 88
            Alpha Company - 14, 38, 88
            Delta Company - 14, 38, 56
         2nd Battalion – 6, 12, 14-15, 21, 29, 35, 45, 61, 72, 77, 85, 90-91, 93, 109, 110
            Headquarters - Captain Graham – 14, 38, 43-44, 52, 88
            Fox Company (assigned) 2nd Platoon - 6, 14, 29, 35, 36-37, 39, 41-43, 50-51, 70, 77
            Fox Company (assigned) - 14, 21, 29, 62, 75, 83, 86, 88, 92, 107-108, 110
            Hotel Company - 51
         3rd Battalion (Maneuver groups for III, MAF) - 13, 14, 23
         3rd Battalion - Lieutenant Colonel Esslinger - 13, 14, 21, 23, 25
                Lieutenant Colonel Webster (later) - 13, 25, 33-34, 36
            India Company – 5, 14, 27
            Lima Company – 14, 27
            Mike Company – 14, 27
      7th Marine Regiment – 11, 14, 55, 59
         1st Battalion - Lieutenant Colonel Jackson - 14, 59
            Delta Company - 14
            Echo Company - 14
         2nd Battalion – 14
            Echo Company - 14
   2nd Division - 71
      2nd Battalion Reconnaissance - 71
         Alpha Company - 71
   3rd Division - 5, 72, 85-86, 109
      9th Marine Regiment - 5-6, 72, 85-86, 109
         3rd Battalion - 5-6, 72, 85-86, 109
            India Company - 2nd Lieutenant Bobo - 5, 72, 85-86, 109

V

Vanbuskirk, Private First Class Gregory N. - 77
VC - 5, 12, 16, 31, 51, 111
Verena, Corporal Ted - 35, 78
Viet Cong - 1, 2, 5, 11-12, 15, 22, 33, 35, 39, 63, 90. 106

W

Wainscott, Private First Class Larry D. - 77
Wall, Lance Corporal Timothy L. - 79
Weed, Private First Class James A. - 75
Westphal, Corporal Jereld - 38-40, 75
Woods, Corporal Lloyd - 81

Y

Yeutter, Lance Corporal Daniel J. - 35, 77
Young, Jr., Private First Class Byron - 78

Made in the USA
Charleston, SC
04 July 2014